GRENIER AIR BASE:

A BEACON ON THE HOME FRONT

LEAH DEARBORN

GRENIER AIR BASE
A BEACON ON THE HOME FRONT

ISBN: 979-8-35097-426-3 (soft cover)

ACKNOWLEDGEMENTS

THIS BOOK WAS NOT WRITTEN IN ISOLATION AND could not have been done without the support of the community of volunteers, donors, staff, and visitors at the Aviation Museum of New Hampshire. Thanks to everyone who stopped by my office to tell me a story, who gave me a call or emailed me with a lead.

A few individuals who contributed to this project include lead archive volunteer Steve Heffelfinger who served as an early reader of the manuscript and oversaw the invaluable digitization process of the *Beacon* as well as the rest of the archive team who consistently brought me articles, documents, and photos throughout this research process. Thanks also to two writers who have already produced work about Grenier: Aurore Eaton and Ed Brouder. Thanks go to Rick Dekostic, Tom Hildreth, and Dan Rothman of the New Boston Historical Society and historian Brian Lindner, Scott Guilbert, Bill Soule, the Tilton Veterans Home, Bob Lacroix, Paul Scarlett, Genevieve Stannard Rowell, Keith Gibbons, Dick Duckoff, Daniel Kelley, Lee Hauenstein, Ruth Mattingly and Cathy Hawkins, Bill Harrell, Richard Sansoucie, Carl Stidsen, and Harvey Cook for sharing your memories and resources with me.

If you do not see your name directly referenced, rest assured that your insight did contribute to our growing collection of knowledge about the history of Grenier Air Base. This project is an ongoing one that does not end with this book, as the Aviation Museum will continue to solicit the stories and memories of those who have a connection to the base.

LEAH DEARBORN

Thanks to the Manchester Historic Association, the World War II Museum of New Orleans, the Archives Department of the Smithsonian Air and Space Museum, the North Atlantic Aviation Museum, the National Museum of the Mighty Eighth Air Force, the New England Air Museum, the New Hampshire Historical Society, and others for helping me track down the remnants of Grenier and for checking your collections even if there was nothing to be found. Thanks to the Wright Museum of World War II for giving me a platform to promote this project.

This book also could not have been written without the investment of those who supported it with a great deal of faith and enthusiasm, including the entire membership base of the New Hampshire Aviation Historical Society. Thanks to the board of directors of the Aviation Museum of N.H., who supported this book from its beginning, and to Executive Director Jeff Rapsis for stumping for the project at our annual gala and overseeing the duration of the writing process. The publishing costs of this project have been generously covered by a grant from the Cogswell Benevolent Trust and its trustees: Peter G. Kachavos, MD, Mark A. Northridge, and Charles S. Goodwin. Thank you to Thomas W. Haas for providing the funding to launch the writing and research phase of this book. The following contributors also made the writing of this book a reality:

Earl Rinker III

Thomas and Stephanie Lewry

Bob Hough

Pat and Jaye Duffy

Jeffrey and Susan Rapsis

Lois Dziergowski

James Tamposi, Jr.

Joanne Greene

Christopher Nisco

Christopher Feinauer

Jodi Savage
Wendell Berthelsen
George Brome
Richard Ludders
Matthew Nihan
Gale Furey
Andrew Fournier
Frederick Kocher
Jeffrey Sullivan
Gerald Moore
Ralph Dionne
Carl Rapsis
Kathleen Sullivan
Ashley Holm
James Schou
Sherree Tocci
Frank Tocci
David Spurrell
Brent Hawkins
Shana Hawrylchak
Deirdre O'Connor
Jody Reese
Al and Glenda Fischer
David and Gail Colglazier
Don Bourassa

And one last thanks to my husband, Christopher Nisco, who listened to me talk about World War II and the Cold War throughout our wedding, honeymoon, and the purchase of our first home.

PREFACE

VISIT THE AVIATION MUSEUM OF N.H., AND YOU'LL find a map that was salvaged from Grenier Air Base sometime after its closure. It's an ordinary National Geographic world map but encased in a heavy wooden frame that appears to have been pried off a wall. Across the top, it's labelled "N.H. Air National Guard."

Straight black lines radiating from Manchester, New Hampshire, have been added to the map. Each line represents an N.H. Air National Guard mission from Grenier to a far-off location. The lines extend across the globe—over the Atlantic to Europe and Africa, down to South America, and across the Pacific to Asia.

Grenier Air Base operated from 1941 to 1966. The map is evidence that what happened there was important. The map shows that Grenier, and the people who served there, played a role as the US military expanded to meet the challenges of World War II, and later the Cold War, in virtually all parts of the globe.

During Grenier's quarter century in existence, tens of thousands of service personnel were stationed there or passed through the base. Hundreds of buildings were erected, from humble barracks to sprawling aircraft maintenance hangars. People from all over the nation trained together for dangerous missions that would take them far from home.

The base boasted its own hospital, church, security force, newspaper, and even a movie theater. Its kitchens served thousands of meals per week. At the height of World War II, hundreds of flights a day landed or took off from its runways—some carrying troops destined to never set foot on US ground again.

And today, it's all gone.

The barracks, the hangars, the hospital—all were abandoned after the military left. The buildings were later torn down to accommodate the growth and development of today's Manchester-Boston Regional Airport. Visit the airfield today, and you'd never guess that it was once home to a busy and important military base.

So, this prompts a question. Shouldn't there be a marker or a monument somewhere?

Yes—and efforts have been made. Even in the base's early years, when the nation was still gearing up for World War II, designs were drawn up for a statue to be erected in appreciation of the sacrifices made by those who served here.

Alas, as the war effort intensified and then concluded, nothing came of the plans.

Not even the "Grenier" name would endure. After the military left, city officials renamed it "Manchester Airport" in the 1970s. An oil portrait of the field's namesake, Lieutenant Jean Grenier, was damaged in a terminal fire and removed; a restored version is preserved in the archives of the Manchester Historic Association.

Still, as the decades rolled by and the buildings vanished, the desire to remember Grenier Air Base persisted, especially among those who had served there.

Consider Peter J. Moulis, a Manchester resident who in 1989 received permission to plant a magnolia tree near the airfield's former main entrance, at the junction of Airport Road and North Perimeter Road.

Moulis, a Manchester native and retired letter carrier, served during World War II in the US Army Air Corps. As a member of the Eighth Air Force's 446th Bombardment Group (Heavy), Moulis received a Purple Heart for "wounds received in action against an enemy of the United States on 21 June 1944, while participating in aerial flight over enemy occupied Continental Europe," according to records in the Aviation Museum's archives.

Moulis was discharged from military service at Grenier, and he later delivered mail on the base, making him part of the Grenier story. Many years later, he resolved to plant the magnolia tree in remembrance of all those who passed through Grenier. The location was chosen to be right below the rise where B-24s would park before heading into combat overseas during World War II.

Alas, in subsequent years, the entire intersection and the surrounding area was completely dug up and reconfigured during a boom in airport passenger traffic. In the early 2000s, a new retaining wall was built, the intersection with Brown Avenue was altered, and traffic signals were installed.

Moulis died in 2007 at age eighty-four. A few years ago, after reviewing his papers in the Aviation Museum's archives, we went looking for the magnolia tree. It was nowhere to be found.

That's why the Aviation Museum of N.H. has published this book. Even the most firmly rooted monuments can be fleeting. To keep the past from fading completely, it's up to us to actively seek out the memories of those who went before us and share them with new generations.

We hope this book about Grenier Air Base and the people who served there can help fulfill that ambition.

Jeff Rapsis, Executive Director
Aviation Museum of N.H.

CONTENTS

INTRODUCTION

AN EAR INFECTION ALMOST CHANGED THE course of Sergeant Edward D. McKenzie's life. It was late winter of 1944, and the nineteen-year-old native of Plaistow, New Hampshire, could feel pressure building up in his right ear as he and the rest of his B-17 crew circled the Boston skyline in their unpressurized cabin, looking for a safe landing area. They had already attempted earlier that day to land at Grenier Air Base in Manchester, New Hampshire, the first stop on their journey to the European theatre of war, but had found that base socked in by poor weather. They were diverted to East Boston Airport[1] where the clouds were just as bad, forcing the crew to turn around once more back to Grenier as the weather began to clear.

Ignoring his growing ear discomfort after the aircraft changed direction a second time, McKenzie, a ball turret gunner, helped the pilot navigate a landing at Grenier, flying just above the civil defense aircraft spotting station in Atkinson where, two short years ago, he was a high school student reporting for three shifts a week to scan the skies with his binoculars for enemy aircraft. Now, fresh from training, McKenzie looked at his home state with new eyes.

He later reminisced of the scene below as the crew descended: "The Grenier air base looked totally different from those I had been used to in western states. The barracks were on pine-covered hillsides above the runways and the flight line, and there was a light cover of snow on the ground. Manchester lay just beyond, with no building taller than the city hall on Elm Street."[2]

Each crew member on the B-17 had been issued a tropical survival pack and ordered to fly the Southern Route to England by way of Brazil and then up through the African continent. But these were decoy orders meant to throw off any Nazi spies who might be paying attention. The crew's *real* orders were to fly the Northern Route—first stop, Grenier Air Base.

Once the crew finally disembarked at Grenier, McKenzie and the others were driven by a Jeep to the transient combat crew quarters for what was meant to be a single tense night before departing for the dangerous adventure that lay ahead of them in England and beyond. McKenzie managed to keep quiet about his ear pain until this point, but in the night, Waist Gunner Bill Hamilton jostled him awake and told him he was talking in his sleep and "if I didn't knock it off, he would put me out in the snow."

The irritated Hamilton woke up another crew member from their group, and together, the two men dragged McKenzie to the base hospital to have a physician take a better look at his ear. When they arrived and released the young ball turret gunner's arms, he fell to the floor, which convinced the initially skeptical corporal on duty that McKenzie wasn't merely trying to get out of serving overseas and that he needed some aspirin and a hospital bed. It turned out that the pressure building in his ear all day was a ruptured eardrum that was now infected.

Satisfied that he would no longer disrupt their sleep, McKenzie's crewmates left him to return to bed, noting that they would probably leave for England in the morning without him and would need all the sleep they could get. Desperate not to miss the flight with the rest of the crew, McKenzie tried unsuccessfully to leave his bed and follow them, not willing to accept that he was going to be left behind.

But fortune had other plans for Edward McKenzie. The next morning dawned, and instead of watching the other men take off, McKenzie awoke to witness the pilot of their B-17 being rushed into the hospital as well with acute appendicitis, delaying their departure by another week. "What a wonderful guy, to make a sacrifice like that for me," McKenzie reflected later.

Not everyone would agree that this twist of fate was "lucky," as the war was just beginning for this crew of young men, with many dark moments ahead. In the 1990s, McKenzie wrote a remarkable memoir of his service, titled *Boys at War, Men at Peace*, which is the source for the exploits connected to the 326th Bomb Squadron of the 92nd Bomb Group featured throughout several subsequent chapters of this book.

On the winter day when they were given permission by a base doctor to fly out for Europe, however, the young crew members of the 326th were filled with anticipation as they prepared to leave Grenier. This was what they had trained for. McKenzie crawled into position in the waist hatch, and the engines of the B-17 came alive.

"Welcome aboard, you malingerers," announced their copilot for the trip. "Now let me fly y'all to where the war is!"[3]

Soon the bomber carrying McKenzie and the rest of the crew was a dot in the New Hampshire skies, one of hundreds undertaking the long freezing journey into the unknown of combat by way of Labrador and Iceland.

When passengers at Manchester-Boston Regional Airport stand in line for a coffee or wait for their boarding group to be called, most have no idea that they're looking out over what was once Grenier Air Base—a primary staging point for heavy bomber crews like McKenzie's, headed ultimately to Germany or North Africa, or anti-submarine groups scouring the Atlantic coast for Nazi vessels. World War II may seem like a distant memory to anyone flying out of New Hampshire on a trip to Florida or watching an Amazon freight shipment take off, but the history of Grenier provides a glimpse into a time when global conflict reverberated uncomfortably close to home.

The lifetime of Grenier Air Base took place within a relatively short span of twenty-six years. It began roughly in 1940 when the land that is now Manchester-Boston Regional Airport was claimed by the War Department for exclusive military use, and it closed in 1966 when the remaining troops relocated to what is now Pease Air National Guard Base.[4]

Among other things, Grenier was a long limb of the Allied war apparatus, directly supplying troops, aircraft, and supplies to the European and North African theatres of war during World War II. According to local historian Tom Hildreth, a deluge of transient combat aircraft poured into Manchester in June 1944 just as Rome was overtaken by the Allies and the beaches of Normandy were swarmed by thousands of soldiers during the D-Day invasion. During Grenier's heyday, over 500 tactical aircraft arrived per month, with a one-day high of 107. These bombers consumed hundreds of thousands of gallons of aviation fuel, and the maintenance activities in support of these planes accounted for more than 22,800 man-hours.[5]

At the outset of World War II, the Air Force was known as the US Army Air Force. It hadn't yet separated out from the Army and was undergoing major structural changes and a massive expansion effort. In just six years, the strength of the US Army Air Force in World War II would rise from 26,500 men and 2,200 aircraft in 1939 to 2,253,000 men and women and 63,715 aircraft in 1945.[6]

Grenier Air Base provided final training for over 51,000 crew members in more than 9,000 B-17s, B-24s, and other combat aircraft.[7] The first American air crews to drop bombs on German soil were trained at Grenier, and in 1942, Grenier Field became the final training facility for the US Eighth Air Force.[8] Bearing these facts in mind, one would expect that such an air base, even if not the largest in the country, would leave a broad footprint behind. After playing a strategic and vital role in World War II, Grenier continued to serve as a key military site during the Cold War. You might also assume that such a large military presence would leave a wide wake after its closure in the form of government documents and artifacts. You wouldn't expect to receive email after email from other museums and historical databases calling Grenier a virtual ghost.

"I'm afraid this isn't 'fall down the stairs' exciting," began one message from the National World War II Museum in New Orleans about everything a search of their collections turned up in relation to Grenier: two pages of orders, a letter from a spouse, a short note written by a captain at Grenier to a Patricia T. Morris instructing her to call the operator in Garden City, New York, regarding the first call she received from her husband from overseas, possibly Germany. "Patty--this is it. Call operator 774. Garden City, N.Y."

These are the little clues that provide a breadcrumb trail of information back to Grenier—snatches of memories and notes on old photos and postcards, the remembrances of a groundskeeper on the base, or the daughter of a man who delivered laundry to soldiers. A large portion of the first-person memories in this book come from residents of the area who were children at the time, who rode their bikes out to downed aircraft or dared each other to sneak on to the base, or even picked up unexploded ordnance off the side of the road.

Other record inquiries produced equally narrow results or nothing at all. The crash of a B-24 in Epsom, New Hampshire, that departed Grenier and killed ten servicemen on their way to Europe yielded zero records or official accident reports from the Air Force Historical Research Agency, yet it was documented in the regional news reports of the day; the terrain was so rural that a road had to be forged up a mountain to recover the bodies.

It's puzzling. How could such a full military installation rise practically overnight, funnel thousands of aircraft and troops into various theatres of war, then face almost total erasure only decades later? World War II is comparatively recent history, from a time when much was documented, and there are those among us who still remember its events or are only a generation or two apart.

There's more than one explanation for why documentation from the World War II era can be difficult to find. Some fault may lie with a massive blaze that tore through the National Personnel Records Center in 1973, destroying approximately 52 million service records of personnel from every military branch, but hitting the Army and Air Force the hardest.[9] Secondly, those who lived through this time period are quickly passing from our midst. Fewer than 389,000 of the 16 million Americans who fought during World War II remain.[10] If not collected soon, their stories will be gone forever.

The war was a global experience shared not just by soldiers but by everyone who felt its impact—in many cases, very young adults and children. As a result, there has been huge variation in the documentation of memories. The last of the Grenier Air Base military buildings, swiftly erected to house the hundreds of military personnel funneled through during World War II, met their demise in the 1990s. All that remains are a collapsing former guard hut, several concrete foundations in the woods, and a chapel that was moved offsite to Merrimack, New Hampshire.

A series of photos of Grenier Air Base, donated by the New Hampshire Department of Transportation to the collections of the New Hampshire Historical Society in Concord, show the base after its glory days when the buildings are clearly dilapidated and vacant, with pallets stacked outside, peeling paint, boarded-up windows. One building sports graffiti that says "Buh bye" on the door. Shots of interiors show a drafting table, lots of cobwebs, and insulation.

There's very little to suggest what the base must have been like in 1944 when it was a beehive of activity thanks to its ideal location as a jumping off point to Newfoundland and then on to the United Kingdom where crews would prepare for raids over Germany and elsewhere. These photos of the derelict base are a dramatic contrast to the newspaper headline from the *Boston American* newspaper in November 1941, which declared Grenier an "Air Base Seen as Tops in the Nation." Additional photos show scenes of civilian stenographers on the base getting fitted with gas masks, base nurses of "such high quality" that they "almost make it fun to be sick at the hospital," and a very young-looking staff sergeant straddling a one-ton bomb being loaded into a transport cart with an added note that it was large enough to wreck a city block.

The base rose out of the farmlands of Londonderry and Manchester in a matter of months and rapidly grew to help meet the country's new role in the Allied war machine, only to be ripped down or slowly sink back into the soil until nothing but memories, scrapbooks, and old newspaper clippings remained. When Grenier was still at its most active during World War II, a historical office was opened on the base so that the men and women who served there would not be forgotten and so there would be a record of this place and its role in history. The goal of this office was to write a complete history of the base from its inception.[11] Whether this was ever fully achieved is unclear, but the book you are reading now is meant to serve a similar purpose, albeit many years later and without the benefit of firsthand experience.

This project, however, is not meant to be an encyclopedic account of every man, woman, and aircraft that passed through Grenier. Rather, it is a broad overview that aims to draw attention to a forgotten place and the vibrancy of the people and community it once served. With so few remaining who remember the base in its heyday, it's impossible to provide a completely exhaustive account.

Much of the research in this text is derived from interviews with veterans who served on or near Grenier in its later years, as well as the family members of those who served or passed through the base during World War II, and many locals who watched the base from their backyards. Historical newspapers, especially the *Manchester Union Leader*, were consulted, as well as Missing Air Crew Reports, Library of Congress records, and microfilm files that the Air Force Historical Research Agency was able to provide. A number of artifacts in museum collections, including the Aviation Museum of N.H., also helped to paint a more complete picture of the base.

The first challenge that presented itself in researching this book was the transitory nature of Grenier. Air crews often only stopped briefly before moving on elsewhere. Second Lieutenant Max Hauenstein of the 487th Bomb Group last landed a B-17 at Grenier Field in summer of 1945 on his return home to the US from England, but the only reason anyone knows he was ever there, even briefly, is because he mentioned it many years later to his son, Lee Hauenstein. Much of the history surrounding the field is oral history, and there are undoubtedly many family stories missing from these pages, especially as the soldiers who came to Grenier were from all walks of life and across the country, often dispersing back to their homes after the war.

The second hurdle in writing this book was the amount of time that has passed since Grenier Air Base was established and at its most active. Interviews were conducted with surviving World War II veterans and civilians who lived through the period in New England. These conversations began with the intent to learn more about the workings of Grenier Air Base specifically, but as it was clear that many of the subjects had little or no recollection of the base, a decision had to be made regarding their memories: should pieces of these interviews be left in or removed? Since live interviews with veterans of this period are becoming more difficult to conduct with every passing year, they were left in. Even if they don't shed light on the daily functions of Grenier Air Base or Manchester during the war and after, they do add color to a time that is perilously close to fading away completely; their firsthand knowledge is helpful in bringing World War II to life through the small everyday details that aren't readily available in textbooks or scholarly articles about the broader causes and effects of the war.

CHAPTER 1

WARNINGS IN THE SKY: THE YEARS LEADING UP TO WORLD WAR II

HAVING LIVED OVER A CENTURY, BILL SOULE OF Seekonk, Massachusetts, has a memory that stretches back further than most. While several of his contemporaries recall Pearl Harbor, his memories go backwards from that still, to the moment he watched the German airship Hindenburg pass like a storm cloud over his head as a child in 1937.

"We were in grammar school out in the backyard playing baseball," he said during a phone interview. "We heard the motor going over the trees, then saw the Hindenburg going right overhead with a big black swastika."

The airship went down to Lakehurst, New Jersey, shortly after and met its infamous fate in a fiery blaze, just a few months after taking high-ranking German officials and American politicians on a collective sight-seeing tour of the New England fall foliage.

The young Soule had no way of knowing what the swastika would come to symbolize. In fact, he and his friends had no idea what the Hindenburg was when they saw it fly over their small Massachusetts town. It was an ominous whirring mystery in the sky. It wasn't until he later saw the newsreel footage of the disastrous end of the airship in a movie theater that Soule connected the dots. There was also no way that Soule could have guessed at what was to come over the next decade: a global conflict that would draw millions into its tendrils including Soule himself, who served at the Battle of the Bulge years later.

But in 1937, several important transitions were happening in aviation and in the technology that would eventually be used to wage World War II and set the stage for the development of Grenier Air Base. The Hindenburg didn't just bring about the deaths of thirty-five people; it also heralded the death of the rigid airship industry.

"They were photographing the East Coast and spying," Soule insisted, adding that German dirigibles commonly patrolled US coastal waters during the interwar years.

A *New York Times* article[12] dated July 14, 1936, details a transatlantic voyage of the Hindenburg before her demise, highlighting the tensions and promises of the years when a tenuous state of peace reigned in the Western hemisphere after World War I. In it, Captain Ernst Lehmann defensively denies directing the ship over prohibited regions of England.

"We know all about these special areas and are careful to avoid them," the captain reportedly said in response to spying accusations. "Someone must have invented that story, perhaps someone who might want to hurt us."

The crew list of that 1936 flight also included two men who fought on opposite sides from each other during World War I.

"Both admitted that they had probably shot at each other many times during the war, but that a cup of wine had since passed between them."

The problem with this seemingly benign anecdote of cross-national comradery is that Soule was right about the spying. German intelligence collected information of relevance from the US throughout the latter half of the 1930s even though the Versailles Treaty had banned post-World War I Germany from spying. Wilhelm Canaris was appointed head of the Abwehr, the Nazi military intelligence service, in 1935, and the organization had more than one thousand employees within a few years.[13] If all this seems disconnected from Grenier Air Base, it's because the explosive surprise attack on Pearl Harbor is generally thought of as the entry point of a formerly isolationist US into World War II. However, during the seemingly peaceful interwar years, the dominos were already being lined up for another world conflict to fall into place. The US Army Center for Military History summarizes the myriad of geopolitical fears of the day:

"Across the oceans, the clouds of war began to form again in 1931 when the Japanese seized Manchuria and then defied the diplomatic efforts of the League of Nations and the United States to pry them loose. In 1933 Japan quit the League and a year later announced that it would no longer be bound by the naval limitation treaties after they expired in 1936. In Europe, Adolf Hitler came to power in Germany in 1933, and by 1936 Nazi Germany had denounced the Treaty of Versailles, embarked on rearmament, and occupied the demilitarized Rhineland. Hitler's partner in dictatorship, Italy's Benito Mussolini, began his career of aggression by attacking Ethiopia in 1935. A revolution in Spain in 1936 not only produced a third dictatorship but also an extended war that became a proving ground for World War II."[14]

As a result, in 1935 the US Armed Forces began to receive larger appropriations to improve their readiness for action in the event of another conflict, including the construction of bases. Although still a long way from becoming a reality, the groundwork that led to the need for Grenier Air Base was laid around this time.

Grenier Air Base wasn't the beginning of aviation in New Hampshire; one of the first flights in the state was that of a Burgess-Wright biplane up the Merrimack Valley by Harry N. Atwood on June 19, 1911.[15] This first flight was such a novelty, a crowd of over ten thousand turned out to watch Atwood's landing (with a speed of about twenty miles per hour) in Manchester at the Valley Street circus grounds. For years after the Wright Brothers' first flight in 1903, the airplane was seen as an intriguing but dangerous contraption, which later became associated with the perils of warfare during World War I. Naysayers called Atwood insane to speculate that there would one day be airplanes capable of flying above two hundred miles per hour. A newspaper article from the 1930s reflects back on the earliest days of aviation in the Granite State: "Names of the other early 'birdmen,' as they were referred to in the news columns of that day, have unfortunately not been preserved for posterity. It is unlikely that there were many of them, for the public did not take kindly to flying in its earliest days."[16]

But things in New England started to change with the advent of Charles Lindbergh's famous flight across the Atlantic in 1927, leading to a period when airport infrastructure began to truly take off around the country.

Lindbergh was the biggest celebrity in the world after becoming the first person to fly solo, nonstop across the Atlantic from New York to Paris. Everyone wanted a piece of the man who'd flown so close to the sun and lived to tell the tale, including the people of Manchester. The story goes that Lindbergh was unable to land in Manchester on his tour of the country after his famed solo flight, leading him to touch down in nearby Concord, New Hampshire, instead. The backlash from this incident is what partially spurred Manchester to build its own airport in 1927. The airport built at that time was originally known as Smith Field (possibly named for the nearby farm of H. C. Smith). The first structures at Smith Field were primitive, wood-frame buildings that existed for pilots to get out of the elements.[17]

For the rest of the 1930s, Manchester Airport developed in a sleepy sort of way. There were air meets and flying lessons held on the field. In 1930, Northeast Airways established a presence at the airport, paying a few hundred dollars per year for hangar rental space. It was considered a major accomplishment when a road running directly across one of the runways was closed to motorists (although the installation of a fence around the field was yet to come). Even the press of the time acknowledged that it was nothing short of a miracle that no accidents occurred on the roadway when it was in use while airplanes landed there. The closure of the road, which directly crossed the landing area, was highly advised by a federal airport specialist in September of 1930.

A *Manchester Union Leader* article written later in 1934 talks about the extension of landing areas at the airport by way of clearing 35 acres of brush to provide access to the full 130 acres of airport property. The result was a north to south runway of about 3,000 feet and east to west runway of the same length, for the price of $21,000 in federal funds. As New Hampshire quietly developed, conflict across the ocean was brewing.

The story of Grenier Air Base's name begins far away from Manchester, New Hampshire, in a swirl of heavy snow and fog near Oakley, Utah, in February of 1934. George Siddoway and his two young sons were cutting wood in Weber Canyon in the northern part of the state when they heard the distinctive roar of an airplane engine, not yet a commonplace sound. Siddoway later recalled hearing the propeller as though its blades were revolving close to the ground, but the plane remained a phantom, obscured in the fog. Siddoway and most of the residents of Oakley reported hearing the plane, but no one could see more than fifty to seventy-five feet away in the poor weather.

"That ship is lost," Siddoway commented soberly to his sons.

The noise of the propeller soon stopped altogether.

On a peaceful ranch pasture nearby, normally reserved for grazing sheep, two Army Air Corps officers lost their lives when their Curtiss A-12 Shrike hit the ground at high speed, plowing through snow and two feet of earth. The force of the impact caused the plane to telescope, according to reporting by the *Salt Lake City Tribune*, and crushed the twenty-four-year-old pilot, Lieutenant Jean Donat Grenier of Manchester, between the engine and reserve gas tank. An attempt by ten men to remove his body was unsuccessful. The wreckage was crushed together so tightly that a team of horses had to rip the plane apart to extract the two victims.

The bodies of Grenier and Lieutenant Edwin D. White, twenty-three, (who had been positioned in the rear seat) were transported offsite by bobsled, then eventually on to Salt Lake City by funeral car. Grenier was buried in Mount Cavalry Cemetery on the West Side of Manchester. He was survived by a large

Quebecois family who mourned the young man's loss so deeply, their grief has had ripple effects throughout the decades since and into the present day.

The skies of the early 1930s were still a largely untouched realm, fostering a sense of daring and innovation that fueled what would come to be known as the Golden Age of Aviation. But with innovation comes risk, and mechanized flight was just over thirty years old in 1934—not enough time to effectively minimize the dangers in a completely new method of travel that took pilots and passengers thousands of feet into the air where there was little room for error. Charles Lindbergh had claimed the prestige of becoming the first solo transatlantic pilot less than a decade earlier, but many other firsts in aviation, such as pressurized cabins or regulations requiring aircraft seatbelts, had yet to be achieved. It was the development of airmail in the early years of aviation that led to Grenier's untimely death.

Air mail routes were first awarded to the private industry with the passage of the Contract Air Mail Act (also known as the Kelly Act) on February 2, 1925. By the 1930s, the American public had grown used to faster, more convenient mail, and it's not easy to walk back progress. But that's exactly what happened when a political conflict rose to a boil in the winter of 1934. The unfortunate Lieutenant Grenier met his end during the US military's valiant attempt to take on the duties of mail transport in the years between World War I and II when there were ample pilots but no conflict for them to serve in.

The project was dubbed the Army Air Corps Mail Operation (AACMO), which resulted in sixty-six crashes and twelve pilot deaths over the span of only a few months. Famed World War I aviator Eddie Rickenbacker flew the final commercial air mail flight and called the plan "legalized murder."[18]

The tangled knot of the AACMO had begun to form four years earlier when then-Postmaster General Walter Brown held a series of closed meetings later called the "Spoils Conference" with airline officials that focused on pressuring smaller independent airlines to merge into larger entities. The intent of this as advertised by Brown was to set the stage for healthy competition that would create longer and more numerous routes.

This plan backfired spectacularly when it was reported in the press that Brown was giving routes to larger airlines whose bids cost triple that of their smaller independent competitors. An investigation spearheaded by Senator Hugo Black of Alabama charged that Postmaster Brown was awarding airline contracts not for the benefit of national interests but his own personal interests, in other words to companies he owned stock in. Against a background of crippling economic depression, unchecked government spending smelled especially foul. After Black produced several damning reports linking air mail stock prices to contract awards, Brown's successor, Postmaster General James Farley, decided to cancel the contracts with private airlines altogether.

At this point, we circle back to Lieutenant Jean Grenier of Manchester. When Farley ended the private contracts to deliver the mail, the US Army Air Corps was asked to pick up the slack and fly mail routes for the first time since World War I. Military leadership, believing the Army Air Corps was up to the task, agreed to the challenge, and the Air Corps began delivering mail across the country starting February 19, 1934. Pilots were blindsided at the time and accurately predicted casualties. This might seem a bit odd to the twenty-first-century observer. Why would military pilots see such perilous difficulty in such a benign task as mail delivery, especially when they'd done it before? What about this order caused veterans of warfare to balk?

One reason for trepidation was that Air Corps aircraft at that time were designed for daytime, clear weather use, and had very few instruments. The vast majority of aircraft used by the Army Air Corps had open cockpits, which was particularly problematic considering that the winter of 1934 brought some of the worst flying weather in years, if not decades. Compounding these issues, many of the pilots had very limited flying experience in bad weather over unfamiliar routes with heavy loads and were generally quite new to flying.

Meanwhile, without much guidance or in some cases even basic equipment, military pilots had a limited time to familiarize themselves with their routes, flying whatever aircraft were available at the time. Grenier, a former co-captain of the University of New Hampshire's boxing team, had only recently made a full recovery from breaking his neck in two places while diving into the Merrimack River. Multiple sources reported that only his "excellent physical condition" allowed the young man to pull through.[19] Not content to linger at home, he joined the 3rd Attack Group of the Army Air Corps as soon as he was fit enough to pass the physical exam. When his fatal crash took place, Grenier hadn't even officially started delivering the mail yet; he was just getting to know the route that he would be flying, which stretched from Salt Lake City to Cheyenne, Wyo.

On March 10, President Roosevelt was compelled to cancel the order that had taken the airmail contracts out of the hands of the private industry. It came too late to help Lieutenant Grenier who by then had been laid to rest in Cavalry Cemetery in Manchester. By May 1934, every airmail route but one was back in the hands of commercial airlines.

The end of the airmail contract mess in Washington could not bring back the lives of the pilots who had perished in the winter of 1934. But almost a decade later in 1941, when the War Department asked the Board of Mayor and aldermen to recommend names of local people for whom the base should be named, the two that came up were former Manchester Mayor Arthur E. Moreau and Lieutenant Jean Grenier, and the vote to use Grenier's name was unanimous.

In 1939 and 1940, reports started to trickle in that the Air Corps was considering establishing its new northeastern base in Manchester. But after several visits by Army boards to survey the city, the news hit that the base would actually be built in Chicopee, Massachusetts. That wasn't the end of the relationship between Manchester and the Army Air Corps, however. As the Battle of Britain raged overseas, Washington watched Europe with a wary eye and approved an expansion of airfield facilities. Within the same week on October 3, 1940, the War Department announced that the Manchester Airport would be developed as Manchester Army Air Base, with expansion efforts to begin immediately.

The Works Project Administration (WPA) broke ground on October 7 under a $1.5 million allotment for base construction with a goal of occupying the base by January. A special edition of the *Manchester Union Leader* from July 17, 1941, compares two photos of the land where the base was built, taken seventy-two days apart in order to show the contrast between the vacant farm field and the rows of base housing that cropped up only ten weeks later. On January 17, 1941, Waino Brooks of East Jaffrey became the first man from New Hampshire to sign up for military service at Grenier. In May of 1941, the first large troop contingent brought two hundred members from the 33rd Air Base Squadron at Mitchel Field, New York, to Grenier for permanent assignment; the first pay day on the base came that same month and sent checks to five hundred men.[20]

Why Manchester? It was seen as a good location strategically: too far from the coast to be vulnerable to attack by sea but close enough to aid the coast if necessary. Other sources state that the lack of foggy weather compared to parts of New York or Boston was a factor. But there's one name that comes up frequently if you research the early history of the airport: James F. O'Neil. He served on the Board of Recreation and Aviation Trustees in the 1930s when some of the land was still a golf course. Armed with only a high school education, O'Neil rose to prominence as the Manchester chief of police and then as the national commander of the American Legion. The *Boston Herald* lauded him in the 1940s as the answer to New England's "drought of outstanding men." O'Neil enlisted in the Army to serve as Mexican border control in 1916 through 1917 and reenlisted upon his return to New Hampshire for service in World War I. When O'Neil did leave the military, it was to become a newspaperman, where he climbed the ranks through local reporting and editing positions.

Local historian Richard Duckoff directly correlates O'Neil's personal connections to high-ranking military officials with the decision to build the base in Manchester. According to author Ed Brouder, O'Neil was Lieutenant Bob Fogg's passenger on the first flight to take off from Manchester Airport in 1927. He became the chairman of the New Hampshire Aeronautics Commission in 1941, the same year that construction began on the new Army air base.

Across the Atlantic, Britain was weathering heavy bombing by German aircraft at this time in a sustained period of attack known as the Blitz. About two weeks before the first significant influx of troops arrived at Grenier, the City of London suffered its highest nightly casualty figure. On the night of May 10, 1941, over seven hundred tons of high explosives and more than eighty tons of incendiaries were dropped. More than two thousand fires were started, and over thirteen hundred people were killed, more than sixteen hundred seriously wounded, and twelve thousand made homeless.[21] With the future of the war a blank page, it prompted the question from many Americans, particularly on the East Coast: could we be next?

Following the outbreak of World War II, Air Base Commander Colonel John I. Moore wrote apologetically to Lieutenant Grenier's mother that no formal dedication ceremony could take place, a decision she seems to have disputed as a ceremony was in fact held three weeks later at a site now known as Grenier Field. Mayor Wilfrid LaFlamme and the aldermen approved a $400 appropriation for a dedication plaque that was put on hold owing to the wartime metal shortage.

After years of delay, the plaque was finally presented in September of 1949. Grenier's bronze plaque was displayed in the Manchester Airport terminal until shortly after the new terminal opened in 1994 when it was moved to storage. In 2002, members of Grenier's distant family who had remained in Manchester went looking for the plaque and couldn't find it. Their persistence eventually resulted in a rededication ceremony for the plaque at the airport. The episode is remembered by Stephen Shea, son of Claire Shea, who was Jean Grenier's second cousin. Shea, who has worked at Manchester Airport since 1998, said Claire insisted that he and his sister know the whole airmail story from front to back since they were children.

Claire Shea had a point. The area surrounding the former air base is the site of many memorials that have been torn down or worn away or, in some cases, were planned extensively but never came into being. That's true of the base itself.

Only the faintest traces remain of the sprawling complex of barracks, hangars, and other structures that played a crucial role in the nation's wartime defense.

Jean Grenier's legacy and his family's battle to keep his memory alive is a testament to the fact that living advocates are needed to keep the history of the base from vanishing back into the soil on which it was built.

CHAPTER 2

"GIVES PRACTICE BOMB TO CHILD": THE WAR COMES TO MANCHESTER

"WHAT DO YOU WISH PEOPLE TODAY UNDERstood about life during World War II?"

It's not a question that you get a chance to ask every day, given that the youngest service members who fought during the conflict have entered their nineties and beyond.

"What do you mean?" asked Charles Tanguay who joined the Navy at seventeen after tricking his French-speaking father into signing the paperwork that allowed him into the service. He told his parents he needed the signature for school and later ended up with the police on his trail when he didn't come home. "I don't think I quite understand you."

I explained that young people born in the 2020s may never have the chance to meet a World War II veteran and hear their perspective firsthand. What the remaining veterans have to say could help future generations understand what life was like during a time that has been relegated to old photos and film, museum collections, and family letters. But here was a chance to speak with living people. The men in the room seemed to seriously consider this for a moment before offering their memories.

Four World War II veterans were in the room at the New Hampshire Veterans Home in Tilton, all of them well into their nineties or beyond. The October day was cool but seasonal, alternating between rain and sun, with a gentle mist lighting on the tops of the trees near the veterans home, which itself has been around long enough to receive veterans from many conflicts, having been established in 1890 for Civil War soldiers. Outside, a shower streaked the windows with condensation, but everyone inside was too engrossed in the conversation to pay the weather much notice.

"They were ecstatic," Norman Sanborn, a merchant marine, recalled of the G.I.s on their way back home stateside from Marseille, France, a slow smile on his face. "I never saw so much money aboard a ship. Crap games, poker."

Born on a small farm in Rochester in the same room his mother was also delivered in, this experience was a big change in his young life. Sanborn was only sixteen at the time he was briefly shipped out to serve aboard a victory ship at the end of the war.

Partway through the hour, Sanborn drifted off and was wheeled back to his room. After many decades, one could only guess what he might be dreaming of and if he could still see the confetti flying as the war ended at last and the rest of his life was about to begin.

The men in the room mainly served at the very end of World War II. One of them, Winston McCarty, pointed out that it seemed almost ridiculous to call him a veteran of World War II as he didn't actually graduate high school until 1946, the year after Germany surrendered. Gradually, though, it became clear that each of the men had clear memories of the war—not of combat, as they didn't see actual fighting, but of the difficulties of life for everyone at that time, young and old.

William Greene, who eventually moved north to New Hampshire from Dorchester, Massachusetts, was sent abroad to Japan while he served with the Air Force in the late 1940s. But many of his recollections predated his service, when air drills were a regular occurrence in his neighborhood. He recalled when each house had to keep a bucket of sand and a flashlight at the ready in case of a firebombing.

McCarty noted that there were lookout stations scattered throughout the state of New Hampshire that reported on any unusual activity. Soldiers were positioned in the countryside to guard the railways and bridges of the North Country.

"Butter was rationed, sugar was rationed—all the things my mother liked," Greene remembered. He said he could see why some people at the time thought the Allies weren't going to win the war. It was by no means a done deal at the time, after all. "For the first three years, we were losing. Then things started to go our way . . . I had great faith in our country and our service people."

He said the war made him the way he was. With all the grown men overseas, he had a chance to take on leadership roles he never would have been offered otherwise as a teenager. In a show of patriotism, he and his mother worked together at a factory making parts for Army, Navy, and Air Corps vehicles.

"Even the fuel for your house was rationed," said Tanguay. "Everything. I had it better out in the Navy than civilians. At least I always had good food."

So, the men remembered the war years, but could any of them remember one specific place in New Hampshire? Did they remember Grenier Air Base, located in Manchester?

The name drew blank looks—as it would if you asked almost anyone taking off from the modern airport on the land the base once occupied—but Winston McCarty tipped back his head, squinting a bit.

"I can remember I used to drive up to Grenier," he said, adding that the name jogged a few things loose in his mind. He moved to Derry in the 1950s and would watch the fighter planes and the C-119 Flying Boxcars take off from Grenier. Mainly, he recalled crowds of people who came to watch astronaut and Derry native Alan Shepard land at the air base. But in the years before that, Grenier was much like World War II on the home front: a place where civilian and military life overlapped, sometimes in less-than-ideal ways.

Imagine opening your newspaper to a headline that reads, "Gives practice bomb to child: Taken from range at New Boston; Col. Moore issues warning." That story ran in the *Manchester Union Leader* on January 29, 1942, and it wasn't even on the front page. A student at Webster Elementary School in Manchester brought in a practice bomb given to them by their father as "an object of curiosity." Luckily, the bomb did not have a detonator, as it was one of the first few dropped on the new range at Grenier Air Base. But that would change within the week, and the inactive bombs were replaced with bombs containing two pounds of powder in their heads. That was enough, the article explained, to make their explosions visible from the air to test the accuracy of bombing, as well as to maim anyone who might pick one off the ground.

It was made clear that no other ordnance was to be taken home. However, as "igloos" were being built to store the bombs on the new base, ordnance was stored out in the open, albeit under guard, until the end of January 1942.[22] Unfortunately, the child at Webster Elementary School wouldn't be the last person to get uncomfortably close to a practice bomb from Grenier. Vernon Wilkins, an eighteen-year-old University of New Hampshire student, suffered serious injury after picking up a "dud" aerial bomb that landed on the open range, which was filled with "only" two pounds of powder.[23]

One of the side effects of having an air base in the community was that there was a need for a place where practice bombs could be dropped. As a result, the New Boston bombing range was developed near Joe English Hill. In a letter petitioning the government for use of the area on September 5, 1941, Colonel John Moore, commanding office at Grenier Field, wrote, "The nature of the terrain around the pond is such that aerial bombing thereon would offer the elements of surprise, concealed approach and navigation to a point." Moore added, "It is believed that Joe English Hill (altitude 1,245 feet) would be a satisfactory stop for any ricochet bullets from ground machine gun targets."[24]

The bombing range in New Boston has its own history that runs parallel to Grenier's and beyond, as the land is still under military control, specifically by the Space Force since 2020. Many locals tell stories of near misses close to the range, including Wade Covill who grew up in Weare, New Hampshire, and whose father was logging near the bombing range in the late 1940s. On a day when he believed that no bombing was taking place, the twelve-year-old Wade made his way by bike with a fishing rod out to the pond on the range.

He would later write in an email to the New Boston Historical Society, "Don't recall a gate, but if there was one, it was open (I think). Anyway, I got to the pond. Could hear heavy equipment working somewhere on the other side of the pond, but fortunately beyond my line of sight. I was on a shoreline devoid of vegetation, lots of junk littering the ground. Little canvas covered frames positioned about the area, looking much the worse for wear. The shoreline was easy to fish as it was pretty torn up. I caught a nice pickerel on my second cast, and thought I was going to have a great day, when I looked up at the hill between me and Manchester.

"Diving straight toward me were three P47s in full attack mode. Thank God they didn't fire, with this dumb kid standing in the middle of the target area. Needless to say I didn't stick around to see what might happen next. In retrospect I doubt it was intended to be a live fire exercise, with work crews nearby. Little did I consider how much unexploded ordnance I must have tramped on. (Didn't our stuff always work?) Most of all, I still remember quite vividly what it feels like to be in the sights of three P47s on a strafing run!"

Other close calls with civilians occurred on or near Grenier Air Force Base besides those that involved explosives. In one instance in December of 1942, two "lightly inebriated" Londonderry men tried to gain access to the base, resulting in their detention and interrogation.[25] It was considered lucky that they weren't shot, as guards were under orders to shoot any intruders in the event that they failed to heed verbal warnings. The country was at war, base commanders emphasized, and no chances could be taken. This was a new reality, and military operations were suddenly thrust into close proximity to churches and schools, farms, and local businesses. Sometimes these two versions of wartime America cohabited peacefully, and sometimes there were painful lessons learned (for example, never approach a burning plane carrying a payload, warned one "Major Black" in a separate article about the perils of getting too close to crashed aircraft from the base).

During World War II, the US suffered an estimated 418,500 combined civilian and military deaths.[26] But numbers don't tell the full story of how World War II irreversibly altered life and the civil order at home as well as the position of the US on the global political stage. No one was excluded from the influence of the war; even children did their part, participating in plane-spotting games to help identify enemy aircraft. The conflict touched the most mundane areas of life. A message from the New England Telephone and Telegraph Company, found inside a matchbook cover from Grenier Field, explains that, "because copper is being used for shells instead of telephone lines, it's necessary to be brief on phone conversations to avoid jamming the lines."

Today, the outcome of World War II is written in stone. That was not the case in the early 1940s when a victory by the Allies was by no means assured and the fear of the average citizen was palpable in every newspaper. Declassified documents show that commanders at Grenier Air Base in Manchester had plans to protect military aircraft by immediately taking to the air if a land invasion were to occur. Air crews transiting overseas through Grenier were told at the height of the war to remain with their planes overnight to prevent sabotage.

Robert Lacroix, who was stationed at Grenier during the 1960s, recalls conversations with some of the senior airmen on the base who served before his time, during the war. Several claimed to witness German seamen who docked their submarines and came into Boston for a drink. Back at the New Hampshire Veterans Home, Will Greene backed this up with his own memories, stating that, during the war, "we had submarines off our coast like it was going out of style." He said that, at night down in Dorchester, people could see the dark silhouettes of German subs lurking in Boston waters. All of New England was preparing for the worst. Some of these stories are anecdotal, the remembrances of rumors. Many of the nightmares that plagued New Englanders during the 1940s remained just that—bad dreams. But others became all too real for Americans, and even the relatively small state of New Hampshire wasn't immune to the tragedies of the coming years.

There's one line in Bernice Blake Perry's flight logs that stands out in bold-printed ink: "Grounded Dec. 8 1941, acct. WAR." Perry was one of the first women in the state of New Hampshire to obtain a pilot's license in 1929 and the first in the state to receive her commercial pilot's license in 1933, making her one of fifty women in the country to obtain a commercial transport rating. An avid scrapbooker, her logs, diaries, and photos from the 1930s contain images of air shows and family outings, of happy-looking young people learning to fly in the golden days of aviation amidst New Hampshire fields and mountains. It's obvious even from the black-and-white snapshots that Bernice Blake's love of flying was infectious and unstoppable, which makes the effect on civilian and commercial aviation clear. Blake's license was reinstated in January 1942, but her scrapbooks show that she suddenly developed a surprising interest in boats for the duration of the war. She would eventually return to flying as her main focus, but through the early 1940s, parts of the state were closed to civilian air traffic under a newly imposed coastal defense zone.[27]

A glance at the front page of newspapers across the globe from December 8, 1941, reveals immediately why Bernice was grounded: a Japanese strike force consisting of 353 aircraft launched from four heavy carriers, including torpedo planes, level bombers, dive-bombers, and fighters, plus additional heavy and light cruisers, submarines, oilers, battleships, and destroyers,[28] had attacked the American base of Pearl Harbor the day before, with the emblem of the Japanese imperial rising sun spotted on the tips of their wings. The attack killed 2,403 US personnel, including 68 civilians, and destroyed or damaged 19 US Navy ships, including 8 battleships. About half of the dead were on the battleship *USS Arizona*.

The Japanese attack on Pearl Harbor hit the US like a rogue wave, but the truth was that, by that time, a perfect storm of factors at home and abroad had led up to the moment when international conflict became inevitable, both in the European and Pacific theatres of war. Japan was searching for resources to fuel its war with China and, in doing so, captured French Indochina. The US responded by freezing Japanese assets in the States and curtailing Japan's access to oil. The Japanese hope was that, by attacking Pearl Harbor, the US would negotiate for peace. But the attack had a very different outcome, drawing the US into the global conflict and altering the course of the war.[29]

In *The Origins of the Second World War* by A. J. P. Taylor, the author notes how much the starting point of World War II can vary depending on the nationality of the observer: "Russians date it from 22 June 1941, the Chinese from November 1937, the Abyssinians, I suppose, from October 1935, and the Americans from 7 December 1941." He goes on to point to the significance of Pearl Harbor, even if it is not marked as the true beginning of the war by non-Americans: "The American date is the most sensible. The war became truly world-wide—much more so than the first world war—only after Pearl Harbor."[30]

These distant events were felt as far away as New Hampshire, with Pearl Harbor having an instant impact on the new and unprepared Grenier Air Base. All the bombs present when the attack on Hawaii occurred were small practice weapons, and the few machine guns on base had no ammunition. This situation didn't last long, however. The first squadron of A-20 Havoc light bombers arrived to equip the 45th Bomb Group, and large quantities of live bombs were soon stored in the open at Manchester.[31]

Genevieve Stannard Rowell of Chester, New Hampshire, can still clearly recall the day that World War II began. Her family had recently moved from Raymond to Derry, and her family members played their own parts in the war effort. Her father was an air raid warden, while one sister worked in a grocery store at the age of eight to help with the labor shortage. Another sister, Ruth Clemen, went into nurse's training as a cadet nurse. To this day, Genevieve keeps the ration books her family saved.

A news photo taken in 1939 at the airport that would become Grenier Field doesn't show Genevieve, five years old at the time, standing just off camera, but it does show her mother and her aunt standing on the wing of an A-17-A attack plane and smiling broadly for the camera along with their cousin, Second Lieutenant Allman Culbertson from Danville, New York, who was passing through. On the summer day the photo was taken, the air base had not yet been built and Germany had yet to invade Poland, although conflict was looming. Genevieve's cousin Culbertson would go on to rise through the ranks, bombing Nazi submarine pens and witnessing D-Day operations through a bird's eye view with the Eighth Air Force. But on the day that photo was taken, it captured only three happy young people, enjoying a family visit. It was the calm before the storm, a time right before many things were about to change, including the airfield where they posed with the attack plane and the city beside it.

In an audio interview from 2006 preserved by the Manchester Historic Association, Manchester resident Peg Parodi spoke about the impact of Pearl Harbor on everyone around her, conveying a sense of surrealness around the start of the war. She grew up on Bow Street in the city's South End, and the conflict motivated her entire family to join in some form of service, including her own induction into the WAVES (the Women's Naval Reserve).

"I was just shocked, couldn't believe it. We knew what had happened [at Pearl Harbor], but we didn't have pictures yet. Today everything is so instant. It was hard to believe anyone would do something like that."

Congress declared war on the Empire of Japan the day after Pearl Harbor, following President Franklin Roosevelt's "Day of Infamy" speech. In response, Hitler declared war on the US on December 11, 1941, as an ally of Japan. From that point on, not only did the war stalk the minds of Americans through their morning newspapers and radio broadcasts, reminders literally fell out of the sky in the form of downed aircraft from Grenier, as training accidents were unfortunately common in the 1940s when many unseasoned young pilots took to the air.

The war invaded every aspect of life, to the point where even women's stockings came in special "alert" colors for the fall in shades dubbed "candle" and "flashlight" in a nod to the blackouts that blanketed New England at the time. A tiny houseboat on a New Hampshire lake became a floating air patrol station.[32]

World War II may have been waged across foreign seas and skies, but the ripple effects of the conflict could be felt globally, including peaceful New Hampshire. Saturday, September 7, 1942, was not just Labor Day in the Granite State; it was also "New Hampshire in the War Day," as decreed by Governor Robert Blood. Blood asked that cities and larger towns around the state hold "impressive parades" to showcase the unity of the community war effort. This request came in a civilian defense issue of the *Manchester Union Leader*, which also advertised blackout shades, provided instructions on what to do in the event of an air raid, and encouraged readers to buy war bonds—quick glimpses into the fears and everyday needs of the era.

In a section titled "Dos and Don'ts for Air Raids," the same defense-oriented publication sternly instructs the use of sand to put out fires caused by incendiary bombs only if water couldn't be located nearby. It must have seemed like sound advice, given that a bordering article provides the expert opinion that a German attack on New England would most likely utilize the same firebombs that were being dropped on British cities at the time. If an air raid did take place, parents were not to attempt to reach their children's schools but to stay home and away from all windows. They were asked not to call the school either, as the wires would need to be clear for urgent messages by police, fire departments, and air raid wardens.

"This is hard advice," the defense publication acknowledged. "It's not easy to take. But it is for your best interest and the interest of your children."

Grenier's role in the global conflict can be seen in the surprising ties between Manchester and even the most well-known events of the war. Shortly after the attack on Pearl Harbor, General Henry "Hap" Arnold selected Lieutenant Colonel James Doolittle to lead Special Aviation Project No. 1, the retaliatory bombing of Japan, in January 1942. In a 1980 interview, Doolittle would cite three "real purposes" for the raid: "One purpose was to give the folks at home the first good news that we'd had in World War II. It caused the Japanese to question their warlords. And from a tactical point of view, it caused the retention of aircraft in Japan for the defense of the home islands when we had no intention of hitting them again, seriously in the near future. Those airplanes would have been much more effective in the South Pacific where the war was going on."[33]

Lieutenant Eugene McGurl of Arlington, Massachusetts, was twenty-five at the time of the Doolittle raid on Tokyo and had attended three years of college before enlisting. He was trained as a navigator and assigned to the 95th Bombardment Squadron of the 17th Bombardment Group.[34] On April 18, 1942, McGurl participated in the famed Doolittle Raid.

During the Doolittle Raid, McGurl's B-25 successfully bombed its targets in Tokyo and continued on to China where bad weather prevented the crew from finding their prearranged landing fields. The crew, including McGurl, safely bailed out near Chuchow.

McGurl later served as the bombardier of a B-25C bomber assigned to the 11th Bombardment Squadron. In June 1942, he took part in a flight of six B-25s from Dinjan, India, to attack Lashio, Burma, which was under siege by the Japanese, and then proceed over the Himalayas to a base in Kunming, China. The raid on Lashio was successful, and the flight withdrew on course to Kunming at ten thousand feet in a thick overcast sky. Suddenly, three planes, including McGurl's, crashed into the side of a mountain. The others barely missed hitting the ground and suffering the same fate.[35]

Although McGurl did not undergo training at Grenier, it was the duty of Colonel John I. Moore, commanding officer at Grenier, to pin the Distinguished Flying Cross onto McGurl's grieving father. The Grenier Field band played a tribute during a ceremony in McGurl's hometown of Arlington with the missing flyer's two younger brothers and mother also present. As they saluted their fallen comrade, members of the Grenier band must have wondered what their own futures would look like in the months to come.

As the war intensified, more young people from New England found themselves in faraway places around the world, thousands of miles from home and in great danger. Charles Tanguay, one of the veterans interviewed at the New Hampshire Veterans Home in Tilton, described the impact that Pearl Harbor had on his brother, Hervey Tanguay. Hervey volunteered for service with the Army a month after the attack, at the first chance he got.

"He was very patriotic," Charles recounted. "He was my hero."

The last time he ever saw Hervey was when his older brother was home on a brief furlough. While at basic training himself, Charles received word that his brother had been killed in action in the Philippines while fighting against Japanese forces at Cebu with the 182nd Infantry Regiment. He was only twenty-four. Over seventy years have passed, and Charles said he still thinks of his brother every day.

"Everybody had to do something," Peg Parodi told her interviewer, referring to the period of unified patriotism that followed the country's entry into the war. She had to stand by on a waiting list to join the WAVES; there were so many women vying to sign up. "Everyone wanted to serve."

One group at Grenier and across New Hampshire that served as a medium for civilians who wanted "to do something" was the Civil Air Patrol (CAP). CAP began in 1936 under Gill Robb Wilson, a World War I aviator and New Jersey director of aeronautics, who was convinced of another impending war. After further development, the program that would become the Civil Air Patrol was approved by the US Commerce, Navy, and War departments in November 1941, and CAP national headquarters began operating December 1 of that year under the direction of National Commander Major General John F. Curry. Public announcement of CAP and national recruiting commenced on December 8, with perfect timing to respond to Pearl Harbor.

A newspaper clipping from the December 9, 1941, edition of the *Union Leader* reads, "The civilian aviation resources of the state and nation are now being marshaled as a component of the total national defense effort through the creation of an organization to be known as Civil Air Patrol . . . Membership in the patrol will be on a voluntary basis, including both flight and ground personnel, and it is assumed that it will be open to both men and women."[36]

Russell Hilliard, director of state aeronautics, was named the commander of the New Hampshire wing of the CAP.

In January of 1942, when German U-boats began attacking the Atlantic seaboard, the CAP took on a surprisingly daring role for civilian aviators and became submarine hunters. On February 6, 1942, it was announced that the airspace over the North Atlantic would be open season for civilian fliers from the Haverhill, Amesbury, and Newburyport areas. They were good at it too—a year later, at least some politicians were crediting the thirty-five hundred New England members of the CAP with chasing U-boats off the Atlantic seaboard.

"Enemy submarines were operating along the Atlantic seaboard within sight of shore," Republican Hatton Sumners (D-Tex) was quoted at the time. "Sinkings of tankers and cargo vessels were a daily occurrence. Available blimps and subchasers were few. Army and Navy planes were urgently needed on the battle fronts." Sumners went on to describe how the civilian fliers maintained a constant watch over northeastern waters with "their own radios, repair parts, tools, and equipment, starting from scratch to fly their single-motored landplanes over the winter ocean unarmed and with no more protection than their kapok life jackets."

Submarines were reported by CAP flyers as well as vessels in distress. With ingenuity and bravery, this diverse crew of civilian fliers strapped real bombs to their private airships. Perhaps even more incredible, they were equipped with "jim-dandy bombsights that only cost twenty cents" but were "deadly accurate to three thousand feet." These figures are especially remarkable in contrast with the much more expansive efforts required to create and protect the Norden bombsight for use by military bomber crews.

These were not military fliers; they were doctors and salesmen, housewives, and bankers. Some were only cadets, young people between the ages of fifteen and eighteen who were admitted into a youth program beginning in 1942. In

New York, the oldest licensed pilot in the country joined the CAP at the age of eighty-one.

CAP fliers may have been volunteers, but they took on real risk. One news article from 1943 details how the government was accused of failing to provide emergency life rafts and other safety equipment to fliers on anti-sub patrols, resulting in some of the seven deaths of CAP fliers within seven months. There was even a "Duck Club" for members who made a forced landing while over water on a coastal patrol and survived.

There were no restrictions on age for joining the CAP, who were unpaid volunteers who only received compensation when sent on specific missions by government agencies. But this volunteer-based operation did much more than attack Nazi subs. They also ran ski patrols, rescued lost hikers, trained to help fight forest fires in the White Mountains, and flew blood plasma and medical supplies in the event of air raids. The CAP still does many of these things today and boasts more than thirty-seven thousand emergency responders in its ranks.[37]

According to a 1942 article by Philip B. Coan, about 15 percent of the nation's 101,000 civilian fliers had applied for the CAP program by that date. It was an ambitious program meant to relieve the military of some of the burden of the war but also looked ahead to buoy private aviation after the war. It was a relatively egalitarian organization for the time, accepting men and women of all ages. The Plymouth squadron received instruction from Ruth Castandyk, one of the few women in the region operating as a flight instructor at the time, and an "all-girl unit" was set up in Laconia, calling on women to assist in office work but also to fly if they were able.

Bob Fogg, the first pilot to take off from Manchester Airport, was named the Air Corp chief, in charge of CAP units in all six New England states. A news clipping from 1944 mentions the CAP cadet recruiting office was at Grenier Field where training would continue for decades.

CAP pilots logged over five hundred thousand flight hours nationwide during the war,[38] making a huge contribution to the effort and demonstrating that people from every demographic were willing and able to do their part. Today, the Civil Air Patrol is still very active in New Hampshire. The Manchester Cadet Squadron that grew out of the CAP operations at Grenier is one of nine modern squadrons in the New Hampshire Wing of the Civil Air Patrol.

CHAPTER 3

WACS, WEATHERMEN, AND BOMBERS: GRENIER AND THE WAR BEYOND

BY THE EARLY 1940S, THE BARRACKS HAD BEEN built at Grenier, but who was occupying them? Once the machinery of the base was in place, who made its wheels turn? The answer is a long one. There were light and heavy bombing groups, guardsmen, communications personnel, members of the Women's Army Auxiliary Corps (WAAC, later shortened to WAC) who operated radios and weather equipment, mechanics, ordnance experts, and others that churned in and out as units and squadrons were reassigned or merged.

During the years of World War II, Grenier saw its first influx of women servicemembers. Edith Nourse Rogers, a congresswoman from Massachusetts, introduced the first bill to establish a women's auxiliary in May 1941. On May 14, 1942, Congress approved the creation of the WAAC. As an auxiliary of the Army, the WAAC had no military status. Therefore Rogers introduced another bill in 1943 to enlist and appoint women in the Army. President Franklin D. Roosevelt signed the bill on July 1, 1943, and ninety days later, the WAAC was discontinued and replaced by the Women's Army Corps (WAC).[39]

One of the hundreds of individuals who found themselves spending time on the base during the war years was a local teenager named Barbara "Babs" Keith.

Keith began a career on Grenier Air Base during the war, as did her sister, Irene Keith. Both were daughters of a Derry farmer who found their niche on the base in careers that may never have presented themselves if not for the conflict. Barbara was an artist who drew illustrations for the base newspaper, the *Beacon*.

An article in the *Beacon* noted, "Corp. 'Babs' Keith of the Marines visited Sub-Depot this week. 'Babs' will be remembered for her clever drawings of lovely ladies with a style a la Petty. She is stationed in Arlington, Va. and loves her work as a draftswoman so much that she says she wishes she had joined this branch of the service much sooner than she did."[40]

Barbara's artistic services would later be requested in Washington, D.C., where she was asked to take aerial photographs and piece them together into invasion illustrations for planning battles. Barbara went on to have a storied career that included drawing lunar samples from the first NASA missions to the moon. But back in 1943, she was spending her time drawing cartoons to buoy the spirits of soldiers at Grenier Air Base.

"I had one of the first working mothers," said her son, Keith Gibbons. "It did make her very happy in life."

Eldest child Irene trained as a civilian mechanic and a member of the WAC at Grenier before transferring to Westover, Massachusetts, and then on to Missouri. In one photo, Irene is shown gassing up a P-51 Mustang, and it's noted in the caption that she was the only WAC on flying status at Rosecrans Field, something that Keith Gibbons confirmed. Because Irene had her pilot's license, she would sometimes get a shot behind the controls of a military aircraft, a rare opportunity for women at the time.

All across the country, thousands of women dubbed "Rosies" were taking on jobs that had previously been exclusive to men. The character of "Rosie the Riveter" first began as a song inspired by war worker Rosalind P. Walter, a nineteen-year-old from Connecticut who began working as a riveter on Corsair fighter planes at the Vought Aircraft Company.[41] At aircraft factories, Rosies worked in the covering and fabric department, cutting out fabric parts and stitching covers for airplane fuselages and wings, parachutes, and pilot seats.

Others put together the radios for each aircraft or served primarily as riveters and welders. The campaign for getting women into the workforce ran on the messaging that, for every job a woman took on the Home Front, it freed up a man to serve overseas.

But women weren't just helping to manufacture the crucial materials needed to win the war; around 350,000 American women also served in uniform, both at home and abroad. They volunteered for the WAC, the Navy Women's Reserve, the Marine Corps Women's Reserve, the Coast Guard Women's Reserve, the Women Airforce Service Pilots, the Army Nurses Corps, and the Navy Nurse Corps.[42]

The Grenier base newspaper, the *Beacon*, regularly profiled different groups from around the base, picking a member to highlight and publish a little about their background. It might be the aviation squadron or the sub depot or the WACs. A July 8, 1944, edition of the *Beacon* included a "WAC of the Week" segment profiling Sergeant Everne Hazenfield, a member of the first WAC contingent to arrive at Grenier. Hazenfield asked whether the reader recalled "that first dilapidated journey-worn group of Wacs, who traveled all the way from Fort Oglethorpe, [Georgia], in chair cars, sleeping in the aisles, got off the train in Manchester one morning over a year ago?" She went on to describe, "How cool and clean and airy the new barracks looked . . . the thrill of being stationed at an air base, with our dayroom overlooking the landing field. Strangeness of all the red lights down on the line, and the 'beacon' up by the main gate that flashes in our window."[43] She recalls hot dogs in the summer at Crystal Lake as well as the less pleasant memories of gas drills and blackouts.

The WACs and other branches of service offered something that women of previous decades had far fewer chances at, especially if they weren't from a family of means—the war offered the possibility of *adventure*. While newspaper headlines still predominantly called out the accolades and promotions of men, now women had a piece of the pie as well. New Hampshire WACs were traveling all over the country and the world for their jobs. The article "Local Wac Works in Old Italian Palace" described how stenographer and former UNH student Private First Class Louise Casey spent her days in the adjutant general's office beneath one of Maldarelli's frescoes. Identical twins June Charlotte and Katherine Carlson celebrated their joint birthday as they were shipped out to the European theatre of war with the USAAF Air Transport Command after their stint at Grenier.[44]

One *Associated Press* article even recounts how Private First Class Edna Shaughnessy, twenty-eight, of Manchester was one of two female marines to be stranded at sea when their Navy Liberator crashed off the coast of Baja, California. The bomber quickly sank, and the crew of eleven was forced to float for four days, subsisting on clams and raw fish until they were rescued by Mexican fisherman. Not as glamorous as working in an Italian palace, but this story of endurance shows that there was quite a variety in the experiences that women encountered while serving their country during World War II.

In the years since World War II, the Women's Airforce Service Pilots, known as WASPs, have particularly captured the imaginations of aviation enthusiasts. These women pilots were trained on nearly every type of aircraft available in the US military at the time, including the heaviest bombers and fastest fighters.[45] They supported the war predominantly by testing and ferrying planes, but there can be no doubt that they were groundbreaking.

There doesn't appear to be any evidence of WASP activity at Grenier, however, despite its location on a major ferry route for bombers overseas. A call to the National WASP World War II Museum in Sweetwater, Texas, confirmed no recorded trips out to Grenier from their records. However, it's difficult to say with certainty that no such trip ever happened or that the base was never a quick stop for a WASP.

Another group of women on the base were the nurses. An issue of the *Beacon* from January 15, 1944, ran a dedicated nurse's column where Lieutenant Naomi Simon stated, "Well, after prolonged heckling to give with a little information on what the nurses have been up to on the base since their arrival here, we finally broke down and agreed to write a 'column.' We wish to state here and now, that this is not our idea, nor our doings." She made some remarks about nurses enjoying winter skating and expressed enthusiasm that they would be allowed to wear olive drab not just overseas but on the base. "Now we actually look like Army, as well as feel like Army, and this change over from the blues to olive drab, makes us all one solid unit, both in color scheme as well as in spirit."

The issue also included a profile of the head nurse at Grenier, Lieutenant Ella Curtis. She's described as very competent, with a background from a charity hospital in New York. The Army Nurse Corps predated the WAC, having formed in 1901, and women served in nursing roles in earlier American wars, including the Revolution and Civil War. According to recruiting materials from the era, Army and Navy nurses were eligible to earn significantly more money than WACs, WAVEs, marines, or SPARs (the Coast Guard Women's Reserve, more commonly known by an acronym for the Coast Guard motto "Semper Paratus—Always Ready").[4647]

There's a strong sense via the base newspaper that the nurses on Grenier were very busy, with little time for nonsense. Photographs show them emerging from voluminous clouds of toxic gas during test drills on the base, administering medicine or helping with rehabilitative activities. It's clear that their duties were integral to the base and the war effort. In fact, records of the Grenier Station Hospital stored at the National Archives in College Park, Maryland, provide considerable information about how the base functioned on a day-to-day basis during the war years.

In an annual report of medical activities concerning the year 1943, it was noted that the station hospital on Grenier Field provided care to more than just soldiers at Grenier. Military personnel stationed at Saint Anselm College in Goffstown, Saint Paul's School in Concord, and the Army Air Base in Bedford, Massachusetts, also received their care at Grenier. In addition, the flight surgeon's office at Grenier performed all physical examinations for aviation cadets in New Hampshire, Vermont, and the Boston area.

The hospital on Grenier had 125 beds when first built, which expanded to 250 with 88 emergency beds available by the end of 1943. At the time the 1943 report was written, plans for additional psychiatric ward facilities had been submitted and an emergency crash ward, equipped for treatment and burn therapy, had been established. There were total 54 officer and nurse personnel, 149 enlisted personnel in the medical detachment (all of whom received basic and advanced training), and 96 civilians employed by the hospital. Surgery services included a trained anesthesiologist, orthopedic surgeon, urologist, ophthalmologist, gynecologist and obstetrician, and "two capable general surgeons." A request had also been made for a physiotherapist. The first surgery on the base took place in 1941 when Private Adelbert Burke's appendix was removed.[48]

The base equipped a dental clinic with total seventeen civilian and military personnel combined. The report from 1943 also made a case that the station hospital was "admirably situated to serve as a base for air evacuation of troops" owing to its location next to an airport and area hospitals, plus room for flight nurses and convalescent training program that included "woodworking, handicraft, publishing of a Hospital newspaper and similar activity."

The report sheds light on several general quality of life and health concerns on a military base in the 1940s. Food served on the base came from approved sources, which the base veterinarian would inspect. Waste was pumped untreated into the Merrimack River, and drinking water came from Lake Massabesic. There was a full-time civilian exterminator for pest control and a "venereal disease control officer," assisted by "a colored noncommission venereal disease officer." The two were in charge of "monthly inspection of troops, lectures on sex hygiene, motion pictures, the use of posters, maintenance of prophylactic station, the stressing of recreation, and physical exercise." A Venereal Disease Control Board met monthly, on which the base chaplain served.

While the war waged abroad and Americans feared for the security of their home, life marched on as usual, with marriages as well as funerals taking place on Grenier Air Base. The conflict also pulled thousands of young people to the area who likely never would have passed through otherwise. Sometimes the confluence of different groups all together in one place was cause for conflict, but sometimes it was the spark of the beginning of a lifelong relationship. Frances Becker, in a Library of Congress recording, said her life before the war in New

Hampshire was very quiet. Because she had spare time, she became secretary for the Jewish Welfare Board under the United Service Organizations (USO). She would send young women from the USO with cakes and sandwiches out to Grenier every week. She got a call before Rosh Hashanah in 1942 that there were soldiers who were looking for hospitality for the holidays. She said this was easy to accommodate because the Jewish families in Manchester were very supportive of the soldiers and often took them in for dinner.[49]

She described meeting her future husband, Eddie Becker, who was stationed at Grenier for six weeks from Hoboken, New Jersey. As a Jewish person, he felt strongly that he had an obligation to serve. He was initially rejected from the armed services but was determined to enlist and tried again. He was sent to Washington, then on to the European theatre. He wasn't a pilot; he was a dentist and was promoted to captain while overseas. He received a Bronze Star Medal for creating dental equipment while in the field out of discarded plane parts. When he returned from the conflict, one of the first things he did was to propose to Frances.

The locals did what they could to boost the morale of the troops at Grenier during World War II. For Christmas of 1944, Red Cross volunteers on the base helped secretly stuff a full Christmas tree and presents into a B-17 bomber headed for Goose Bay, Labrador. The decorations and presents traveled over one thousand miles, and on Christmas Day, each man on the crew received the much-appreciated gift of a carton of cigarettes (except for the radioman who didn't smoke and was given a scarf instead).

The global seismic shift wrought by World War II upended the norms and shook up the status quo at home, but for every opportunity the conflict created, it stole hundreds away. Folders full of clippings in the Aviation Museum's archives from the 1940s bear the names of those from New Hampshire who were missing in action. Others returned from the war intact but without the innocence they once enjoyed. Childhoods were ended abruptly to work necessary jobs or obliterated entirely by the horrors witnessed overseas.

At the same time air leaders were working to expand air bases in the late 1930s, they were also striving to create an independent institutional structure for the relatively new militarization of aviation within the US Army. The Air Corps, during this period of expansion and reorganization, created a new echelon that would soon become the numbered air forces. In December 1940, the War Department formed the Northeast, Northwest, Southeast, and Southwest Air Districts to help control these tactical organizations. Grenier, of course, was part of the Northeast.

These districts were redesignated in April 1941 as the 1st, 2nd, 3rd, and 4th Air Forces; later, the Arabic designations were changed to the First, Second, Third, and Fourth Air Forces. The Hawaiian Air Force was activated on November 1, 1940, the Panama Canal Air Force on November 20, 1940, and the Alaskan Air Force on January 15, 1942. These air forces subsequently became the Seventh, Sixth, and Eleventh Air Forces.

And then there was the Eighth Air Force, known as the Mighty Eighth, which would go on to become the largest air armada in the world, capable of sending more than two thousand heavy bombers and over one thousand fighter planes on a single mission, but which started out as just seven men with no aircraft in Savannah, Georgia.[50] During the war, the US primarily utilized five types of bombers: the B-17, B-24, B-25, B-26, and B-29.[51] In relation to Grenier, the most referenced aircraft are the B-17 and B-24, both of which were four-engine bombers. The B-24 was capable of carrying eighty-eight hundred pounds of bombs, whereas the B-17 was able to carry only about sixty-six hundred pounds but for a distance of two thousand miles.[52]

The Army Air Force suffered 121,867 casualties during the war, with the highest number among fighter pilots and bomber crew members.[53] In the first two years of US' involvement in World War II, the Army made a purposeful effort to recruit the best and brightest to the Air Force, but by the end of the war, it had more pilot candidates than it could train. A lot of stock was put in the Army

General Classification Test (AGCT), and its top scorers were generally funneled into the Air Force. Notably, only volunteers were accepted for air combat roles; these positions were never filled from a draft. They represented a cross-section of America, hailing from urban New Jersey to the corn fields of Iowa. A search of service records at Grenier mirrors this.

Grenier sent troops to the European theatre of war, often to England before their eventual missions over the skies of France, Germany, Austria, and other countries. Other soldiers found themselves flying through Italy or on to North Africa. Once in England, troops often enjoyed many of the amenities that they would have at Grenier, as documented in a Red Cross document produced about the 388th Bomb Group and their base in Knettishall, England.

"An army station is a community, a city in itself," began the pamphlet. "Overseas, thousands of miles from home, the men of this Station in the European Theatre of Operations, have attempted to make their community as livable as possible... What pictures cannot describe is the immense resourcefulness, energy and talent that went into making our Station 'something like home.'"

The description could be of Grenier, which also had its own game rooms, gymnasium, and movie theater, all the trappings of makeshift comfort. The difference overseas was the proximity of the war, the real possibility of a German raid at any time. Members of the 560th Squadron under the 388th Bomb Group would later be shot down over Germany and held as prisoners of war, having traveled the long journey via a B-17 from Manchester to Goose Bay, Labrador, to Greenland, Iceland, Wales, and England to eventually end up in Stalag Luft 1A in Barth, Germany. Squadron member Raymond Klinke recounted how the Germans at the camp were forever searching for a secret radio that provided BBC news. As a prank during a barracks search, one American bent down and pretended to cover something up in gravel. Other POWs caught on and began to do the same thing, leading the Germans on a wild goose chase from man to man. Klinke didn't find out who owned the radio until after the camp was liberated by the Russians in 1945.[54]

Air Force Combat Units of World War II by Maurer Maurer provides a listing of the combat or tactical groups (including bombardment, fighter, reconnaissance, and troop carriers) that were active during World War II, as well as their various stations. In total, Maurer names the following groups as being active at Grenier: 2nd Fighter, 4th Fighter, 5th Fighter, 48th Fighter, 69th Fighter, 81st Troop Carrier, 95th Fighter, 96th Fighter, 97th Fighter, 310th Fighter, 311th Fighter, 315th Fighter, 318th Fighter, 332nd Bombardment, 359th Fighter, 360th Fighter, 361st Fighter, 368th Fighter, 369th Bombardment, 490th Fighter, and 863rd Bombardment.[55] Newspaper clippings, letters, archival documents, and conversations with the families of veterans also occasionally turn up units not listed, perhaps because their stop at the field was brief.

Without context, however, none of this means very much, as Maurer provides fairly limited details on the actual duties of each group. The 356th Fighter Group, for instance, isn't listed but was directly assigned to Goxhill, England, after their departure from Grenier after an active period in the summer of 1943. They went on to support the landings at Normandy and the subsequent drive of Allied forces across France and Germany. The 356th flew 413 missions between October 1943 and May 1945 and suffered the highest ratio of losses to enemy aircraft claims of any Eighth Air Force Group.[56] When Grenier is referenced as a final stop for American soldiers, the 356th is just one example of how dangerous the reality of war was for these young, often green air combatants.

One of the young men who found their way briefly to Grenier was Marshall Lumsden, originally of Michigan. Lumsden came to Manchester in November of 1942, less than a year after the attack on Pearl Harbor. He was only twenty years old and straight out of flying school, assigned to the 315th Fighter Squadron. In a 2003 *Air & Space Magazine* article reflecting on his experience, he referred to "veteran pilots" as anyone who had logged a few hours.

"In those days before flight simulators and two-seat training versions, we learned to fly a single-seat fighter by getting in it and taking off," Lumsden wrote.[57]

Indeed, military photos from late 1942 document numerous nasty-looking P-40 training accidents in the woodlands and farm fields surrounding Grenier Air

Base. At that point, the 315th had been dropped off in late fall of 1942 and into the winter months in Manchester to prepare for the invasion of North Africa.[58] The twenty-eight pilots, accompanied by over two hundred ground personnel, trained on the Curtiss P-40F. Lumsden confessed that the 315th and Manchester were a bad match, with the group's rabblerousing antics causing some tension.

"We found the city to be rather dull," wrote Lumsden, who later moved to California after the war. "After all, we were a fighter outfit headed off to war, and we were full of beans. We adopted what we assumed to be the raunchy insouciance of Britain's Royal Air Force pilots."

He described spontaneous dogfights with any Navy Hellcats and Corsairs encountered off the coast of New England while training and getting ice fishermen to dive for cover by flying low over New Hampshire's lakes. Within a few months, Lumsden left Grenier for a train station in Boston where his travels took him on to Florida, then onboard a military air transport to Lagos, Nigeria, where Lumsden and the 315th picked up newly assembled P-40s. By May 1943, Lumsden had survived his first combat mission but lost a third of his fellow pilots within six months.

Lumsden and the 315th Fighter Squadron weren't the only troops to move through Grenier on to the front in North Africa. The North African Campaign had its beginnings in 1940 when Italy's fascist dictator Benito Mussolini wanted to expand his African Empire. His forces in Ethiopia attacked neighboring British possessions but, in 1941, were expelled and defeated. Incursions by Mussolini from Libya into Egypt were also met with defeat.

As a result, in February 1941, Hitler sent the Afrika Korps, commanded by General Erwin Rommel, to bolster his ally in North Africa. The German counteroffensive pushed the British back to the Egyptian frontier and kicked off a struggle in the Western Desert that continued for the next eighteen months. British forces, under a succession of commanders, were continually outfought by Rommel. The German Afrika Korps at that time were waging heavy battles east of Tunisia. British forces were reinforced by troops from New Zealand and Australia, but American air power was badly needed to help destroy Rommel's supply lines.

Harold Ray Warren Jr. is an example of why the story of Grenier Air Base is difficult to document; it was a transitory place. Grenier was a stepping stone for service members from all over the country who found themselves in New Hampshire but only for a short time before moving on to other more harrowing experiences. Warren would eventually fly through Grenier and then on to the North African theatre. While his adventures during the war were numerous and took him to far-flung reaches across the globe, his time on the base itself was limited to a few weeks.

However, Warren's diary, located in the archives of the Aviation Museum of N.H., is a great resource for understanding the mentality of the fighter pilot about to embark for a combat zone. He described the difficulty of becoming a flying cadet in the Army Air Force, explaining that, at the time when he joined in 1940, the requirement was to have two years of college or take an equivalent exam. Although he'd been out of high school for four years, he dreamed of flight. He decided to take the exam, and he got in. Harold was sent from Boston with fifty-four other flying cadets to train in Georgia where he learned to fly in a Stearman PT-17.

In his private journal, Warren divulged details of the life of a flying cadet in 1941. He described a "West Point class system" that involved strict discipline and continuous hazing, which Warren said prepared him for the experience of flying in combat. Despite the looming dangers of training and military service, he also wrote of the unbridled joy of flight. "When I made my first flight, it really was my first flight in any aircraft and I was positively thrilled and excited! The only time I was even more excited was when I soloed ten hours later. I knew then that this was my true dream coming true."[59]

Warren moved up the ranks and trained on night flying, precision formation flying, cross country and instrument flying, and flying at high altitude with oxygen masks. After practicing on the North American AT-6 Texan to fine-tune his skills, Warren was assigned to the 52nd Fighter Group at Selfridge Field in Mount Clemens, Michigan. Overall, he described a period of a little over seven months divided between the primary, basic, and advanced schools of training. In primary, students were introduced to the basic elements of flight and expected to solo in thirteen hours or so of training; those who did not were at risk of "washing out."

On June 11, 1942, Warren was transferred with the rest of the 52nd Group to Grenier Field where they were given new P-39s with 175-gallon tanks. The plan was to fly the P-39s to Iceland, then go on to Northern Ireland with B-17s. The 52nd trained grueling six-hour missions around New England in preparation for this plan, but it was eventually canceled.

Unsure where he was headed to next, Warren wrote, "After intensive training in a fighter aircraft, I was about to go overseas to a war zone and combat. That in itself brought anxiety and excitement. I really had no idea what lay in store for me, and being only twenty-three years old, I was gung-ho and curious to learn all about this war."[60]

Warren left Grenier on June 26, 1942, not long after arriving. He was sent to Fort Dix, New Jersey, and from there he boarded a ship to Halifax, Nova Scotia, with five thousand other men. They sailed into the fog after listening to a radio announcement by Hitler that no more American convoys were to be allowed to reach England. By the third day, two other transports were missing. Warren was traveling during the height of the Battle of the Atlantic, the longest military campaign of World War II. The flow of war materials into Great Britain via the Atlantic was the lifeline of the Allied war effort against Germany, one that Germany was fighting tooth and nail to sever. During the first three months of 1942 alone, German U-boats sank more than hundred ships off the east coast of North America, in the Gulf of Mexico and in the Caribbean Sea, making this crossing a dangerous one.[61]

Fog lingered and the ship continued onwards, skipping Halifax altogether. By the sixth day, Warren wrote longingly of his wife of a few months, "Getting tired of this trip. Feeling down and all I think of is how much I miss Dorothy."

On Friday, the tenth day of the trip, an air raid was expected but never came, with no one allowed on the top two decks and British coastal bombers surrounding the convoy throughout the day. Finally, the ship arrived at Liverpool on Sunday, July 12. The next period of time was a lot of waiting in the English rain.

Warren gave a glimpse of life during the in-between times of the war when troops were waiting to enter combat. A week of rations contained five cans of beer, four bottles of Coke, a pack of gum, a pack of Lifesavers, a can of fruit juice, and four candy bars. The waiting was sprinkled with training accidents, as pilots grew rusty during transit. On August 14, 1942, he wrote, "Flew one mission today. Don't see how we can go operational in a month."

He went on to explain that, when the Army Air Corps pilots switched to Spitfires while overseas, it immediately caused accidents, but they were the only planes available at the time. The Spitfire was a "tail-dragger" in contrast to the tricycle landing gear of the P-39 that they were familiar with. The narrower landing gear made landing more difficult, and it required skill and attention to avoid a ground loop, a sharp, uncontrolled change of direction of an airplane on the ground.[62] Although initially unimpressed with the Spitfire, Warren would later change his mind and commended it as the most maneuverable aircraft in use during the war.

As a pilot in the 52nd Fighter Group, Warren would eventually be sent to Gibraltar, then Algeria in November of 1942. In December, he wrote that the British were pushing Rommel to the west, while the Americans were pushing him to the east. As his time in combat dragged on, Warren noted the accumulating casualties from his squadron and was blatantly pessimistic about the outcome of the war overall. He wrote in his journal that, almost nine months after leaving Grenier, he took part in the battle of Kasserine Pass in Western Tunisia, during which Allied forces suffered major losses due in part to a lack of unity by American leadership.[63] It's not surprising that this young soldier was beginning to feel jaded.

The turning point in North Africa had already begun at the battle of El Alamein in October 1942 when General Montgomery inflicted a decisive defeat on the Axis forces. The Americans joined the fight in North Africa on November 8, but that didn't mean that the war became easier.

Warren's diary recalls him eating poorly, slogging through mud, and being unable to shower for weeks at a time. However, other soldiers who spent time at Grenier had dramatically different experiences. In an interview about his service during World War II, James Clem Kraner of Pickerington, Ohio, stated that he only saw enemy troops once throughout the war when a group of Germans was caught trying to mine weather data from the frigid shores of Labrador.

Kraner described watching Hitler's crawl across Europe as a young man, witnessing the capture first of Czechoslovakia and then Poland, thinking to himself that "someone needed to stop him. And that someone would likely have to be the United States." The week he graduated high school in 1940 was the week that Hitler overran France.[64]

Kraner was in college and playing football when his dad called him in and told him about Pearl Harbor. Instead of enlisting right away, he tried to start college; the draft age was twenty-one at the time, and he was seventeen. But in 1942, the draft age was lowered, and Kraner was inducted at Fort Hayes in Ohio. Whereas he was rejected by the Navy because of his eyesight, the Army had no problem with his vision. He noted to the recruiting officer that he was interested in weather and might want to become a meteorologist one day. As a result, he ended up in the 8th Weather Squadron and would be sent from basic training in Miami Beach to the far ends of the earth. But first, he attended weather observation school in Illinois, learning about how to make weather observations and also how to encode the observations so they couldn't be interpreted by the enemy.

He left weather observation training in May of 1943 and was sent to Presque Isle, Maine, where the 8th Weather was originally headquartered before it was moved to Grenier later in the war. Kraner and the other troops knew they were going north somewhere to Labrador or Iceland. They may have been largely trained to make weather observations, but the 8th Weather was armed as well.

"Whatever defense weathermen might provide, we were given a carbine and fifty rounds of ammunition," said Kraner.

They were also given special heavy gloves with holes for their trigger fingers. On June 14, 1943, Kraner flew from Presque Isle to Labrador for an assignment of eighteen months in Goose Bay. Similar to Grenier, Goose Bay was constructed in a great hurry by the people in the area at a higher salary than they were normally paid. The base there was shared between US and Canadian troops and some British.

"Their purpose was to fly the big bombers to England," recounted Kraner.

Pilots who flew in would be briefed and given the weather all across the North Atlantic, including if there were any icing conditions. When weather was bad, they would get planes into the base but couldn't get them out for ten days or more, which would seriously tax the resources of the remote facilities. Understanding the weather in the North Atlantic was particularly important because it fed into France and other battle grounds throughout Europe. When troops went into D-Day, they picked up the front on the coast of Labrador and followed it across the Atlantic. The meteorologists advising Eisenhower were able to make him aware of a weather advantage that the Germans were unaware of, although the Axis also tried to develop a hold in the region for gathering weather data via covert operations.

Kraner stated that Germans used to fly planes out to Iceland, not to bomb it but to read the weather. Germans had planted an automatic weather station through a submarine that used radio to determine pressure and temperature. The Americans intercepted the signal but couldn't find the device to remove it until after the war. Despite the frigid weather, Goose Bay was a key hub that pulled major celebrities of the day to entertain troops such as Marlene Dietrich who came to perform with musical saws.

When Kraner was sent back to Presque Isle in December of 1944 after serving eighteen months, he was then sent to report at Grenier where an extended forecast station had since been built in anticipation of Grenier's new appointment as home of the 8th Weather and the North Atlantic Division Headquarters for the Air Transport Command. Observation and the creation of weather maps were among his duties as part of the efforts to forecast which route was better to transport planes: the North Atlantic route or south across to the Azores.

Weather intelligence was critical not just to generals and high-ranking officers making major tactical decisions but also to the success and survival of the air crews carrying out missions over Europe. Jeff Johnson, a top turret gunner and member of the 458th bomb group 754th squadron of the Eighth Air Force, was one of many airmen who briefly passed through Grenier.[65]

Johnson enlisted in July 1940 before the war officially began and went to gunnery school because pilot training was full. He paid credit to the military weather forecasters, calling what they said gospel in making the in-air decisions to attack a target or pull back.

Johnson also described the perils of serving from the upper turret of a B-24. During one incident, he asked for the radio operator to pass him his flak helmet. While he was bending down to retrieve the helmet, anti-aircraft fire hit exactly where his head had been just seconds before. He would watch superiors check the crew's dog tags before a mission, knowing that their concern didn't bode well for the safety of the crew who were each given tiny maps of the target area made of very thin rubber in case they were shot down and survived. The thinness of the materials allowed the map to (ideally) be hidden in case of interrogation and used by the downed crew member to find their way back to Allied territory.

Missions were not brief. Johnson recalled the longest one lasting about nine hours, while the shortest was about five. It took forty minutes for the aircraft to get into formation, with one plane in the group painted like "an ad for spray paint or something," which was called a "speckled egg" that pilots could easily spot and assemble around. Without pressurized cabins, there were other dangers besides enemy flak; oxygen masks had to come on over altitudes of twelve thousand feet or so. Johnson recalled a ball turret gunner who fell asleep on top of the hose to his oxygen mask and passed out. When crews returned from a mission, they were given a shot of bourbon to settle their nerves. The only time Johnson was ever apologized to in the service was when "they ran out of whiskey" and had to give him "cognac."

In his memoir about the 306th Bomb Group of the 368th Bomb Squadron, Paul Bagley described the importance of Grenier as a place of preparedness. This was where many aircraft received their final outfitting before being sent into combat, making it the last chance to confirm that all systems were as ready as they could be to endure battle. It was important work, with the lives of all crew members on the line. "Attaching all the mounting hardware to the airplane was no easy task. The mechanical crew at Grenier had their hands full setting up the heavy bombers with the defensive shields they would need in battles to come."[66]

Because Grenier was a transient place where many individuals converged from around the country, it was a place of little sentimentality for most. However, for some of the crews who were being briefly returned to New Hampshire for training, it was also one last chance to reunite with family. When service members Bill Witcomb and Norris Hales were sent to Grenier via a course that went directly over Hales' hometown, they were greeted by a crowd of people standing in a field below with bedsheets that spelled out the word "Hello" in salute to the returning fliers in their B-17G. From the cockpit, Hales waved down below to his fiancé, family, and friends.

Many stories about the men and women who passed through Grenier are lost to us. We'll never know a fraction of who passed through and what they went on to experience across the far reaches of the globe. But sometimes, old stories can surface through a descendant, an old newspaper clipping, or a breadcrumb trail of military records.

In the case of Roland E. Bunker, Jr., his name was in a collection of news clippings on New Hampshire aviators, seemingly collected by the military and donated to the collections of the New Hampshire Aviation Historical Society many decades after the war. Bunker is featured in an article without byline, titled, "Blinded by flak, N.H. flier patches bomber, gets back."

A technical sergeant and top turret gunner on a 15th Air Force B-24 Liberator, Bunker was in the lead ship in a raid against the rail yards in Vienna.

It was poor flying weather, but the ship managed to find a way through the clouds where it was met with flak from four-hundred-plus guns. His crewmate, Bombardier First Lieutenant Elton Stinson, dropped the bomber's payload across the yards, then called back to Bunker for a damage report. Hearing nothing back, he screamed through the hatchway and came out covered in hydraulic fluid, essential to the ship's brakes, wing flaps, and turrets. When Stinson hauled Bunker out of the turret, the gunner's face and eyes were bleeding where shattered glass from several flak hits had struck him.

Stinson quickly bandaged his crewmate up and sent him to the flight deck, but Bunker didn't stay there; instead, he tore off the bandages and went directly back to the punctured line to work furiously at stemming the leak. With hydraulic fluid still spraying everywhere, Bunker worked his way down the Liberator with pliers and tape, crimping, applying torniquets, and covering the damaged lines. The heater lines had also been smashed, so Bunker turned the end of that hose and shoved it through a flak hole, not wanting the crew to contend with carbon monoxide poisoning on top of trying to escape enemy fire.

Stinson later told a reporter, "I prayed Bunker had hooked and spliced the correct lines—he was working on the catwalk with the bomb bays open. He ran short of oxygen several times but we had enough to charge the walk around bottles from the main system. But the kid was working more by braille than sight. We circled once and landed. There was enough juice left for one application of brakes. It saved us."

Bunker himself only had a brief comment at the time: "Heroics? Hell no. I wanted to come back alive."

After his narrow brush with death in the skies of Europe, Bunker would go on to live a long life back in New England. He served in the Air Force Reserve as a senior master sergeant at Grenier Field and finished his career working as a jet aircraft inspector at Curtiss-Wright in New Jersey and General Electric in Lynn, Massachusetts, and Hooksett. He was active in the community, with other newspaper articles from the late 1940s focused not on his daring fight for survival while blinded by German flak but as his role as a campaign director for the March of Dimes.

Bunker is one example out of many thousands of "ordinary" people who found themselves pushed to the brink by the war only to discover in themselves a deep will to survive and to help save the lives of others. "Ingenuity" is a word that comes to mind frequently when reading personal accounts of World War II.

Another example of this type of elbow grease detailed in a folder of news clippings came from Sergeant Joseph E. Landry of Pelham, New Hampshire, and Private Harwood D. Jones of Pittsfield, New Hampshire, who enlisted in Manchester and built an airfield in ten days on a rocky island in the Adriatic Sea off the Italian peninsula. As part of a special aviation engineer task force, the men were sent with a landing ship tank (LST) full of bulldozers, graders, compressors, and carryalls to what was then Yugoslavia. They were greeted by Josip Broz Tito's guerilla Partisans who were skeptical that an airstrip could be completed so quickly (or at all) on the island where the most level spot was marked by a rocky vineyard.

Still, Partisans not engaged in nightly guerilla raids helped the US soldiers hack away at the vines and underbrush and to level the area. The nearest Nazi-occupied territory was only eight miles away as they worked through the rain, all the while wearing helmets and carrying guns. Miraculously, the airfield was completed in the ten-day window, after which RAF Spitfires were able to land, refuel, and destroy over seventy enemy vehicles in the first air raid to take off from Yugoslavian territory. Landry returned home to become (aptly) a landscape gardener in the Nashua area.

Another individual caught up in the intercontinental spiderweb of air crews who readied for combat at Grenier Air Force Base was Corporal John "Thomas" Kelley.

His logbook entry from December 28, 1944, read, "Left Lincoln, Nebraska at night in a blizzard and landed next morning at Grenier Field. Most of the flight was made in instrument conditions. At Grenier, we were processed and readied for our trip across (the Atlantic)."

Five days later, the crew lifted off for Goose Bay, Labrador, from which they then moved on to Iceland, then Wales, and finally to England. The trip would take them over a month in miserable weather conditions.

Thomas Kelley, uncle of Aviation Museum docent Dan Kelley, served his first of thirty-one missions on February 19, 1945, over Gelsenkirchen, Germany, on a B-17 Flying Fortress. Victory in Europe (VE Day) was only a few months away, but no one fighting in the skies over Europe would have guessed that. The ferocity of the German defense was startling even in the last days of the war. In March, the Germans were fighting through their own flak, which Dan Kelley likened to running through an active target range.

"It was crazy, just a real fur ball. Planes everywhere, flak everywhere," he commented in an interview about his uncle's service as an engineer and flight mechanic in the 545th Bombardment Squadron (Heavy).

On that first mission, Thomas Kelley's number two engine was knocked out by flak. German jets were able to get within about eight hundred yards of his aircraft, but their guns appeared to jam and they peeled off. The other German jets were scared off by P-51 Mustangs, the legendary fighters of World War II who flew with the B-17s as escorts. Thomas Kelley would later write in his logs, "Those P-51s are handy little guys to have around." On other occasions, his meticulous flight logs would refer to the P-51s as "guardian angels watching over us."

Dan Kelley said his uncle never talked about the entries detailed in his logbook, but he did talk about his love of the P-51. "He really felt that that airplane saved his life," Dan Kelley said.

It wasn't just the P-51 that got Thomas Kelley through the war in one piece, however. On one mission, Second Lieutenant William C. Murphy saved his life twice. Murphy had ordered his crew to bail out of their B-17, which was hit and going down. Everyone else was already gone from the plane. Thomas Kelley walked to his station to bail out when Murphy (the pilot) suddenly threw his kneeboard at him and started to frantically motion for him to come up to the cockpit. At that point, Thomas Kelley saw that his parachute was on fire.

Murphy told him, "Strap your ass in. We're going to ditch this son of a bitch!"

And they did. Thanks to Murphy's flying skills, they ditched safely in the English Channel where the British air-sea rescue found them, probably after sighting the smoke coming from their damaged engines. They were pulled out of the frigid waters just as their plane, nicknamed "The Purple Pup," slipped between the waves to the channel's bottom.

Jay Kelley, Dan's cousin, said of his father and comrades, "They were certainly brave men. It's kind of a miracle I'm even here."

On one mission on April 6, 1945, the 545th Bombardment Squadron was hitting the railroad marshalling yards at Leipzig when, as Thomas Kelley watched in horror, a B-17 that was part of their group went into a tailspin and fell apart after colliding with another aircraft from their group. Thomas Kelley wrote in his log, "If I live to be 100, I don't think I'll ever forget the sight of that B-17 falling earthwards."

On VE Day, Thomas and his colleagues decided to go on a "sightseeing" trip from the air and were amazed at the damage they saw below. The marshalling yards were nothing but a mass of twisted steel. The only thing left standing in Cologne, Germany, was a cathedral—the Kölner Dom—which was captured by aerial photographers as the sole standing structure amidst a city honeycombed by bombing.

Dan Kelley said his uncle didn't talk directly about how he felt flying over the destruction caused by the bombers. "He was probably numb." He added that, reading between the lines, he didn't think there was much empathy left by that point in the war; it had been replaced by resignation. Six decades later, when a B-17 visited the Aviation Museum of N.H., Dan Kelley was struck by the sad thought that their days preparing for the war ahead at Grenier Air Base were "the last time many of those kids ever set foot on American soil."

Dan Kelley said his uncle probably never would have joined the military if it weren't for World War II. Dan's father, Daniel W. Kelley, also tried to join the Army Air Corps, but he was pulled and sent to medic school, serving instead on Utah Beach in Normandy, France, on D-Day. As soon as the ramp on the boat was down, a German rifleman opened up fire. Dan's father was eighteen and had been in combat for sixty seconds before he saw a man's face completely shot away. Dan's father tried to administer aid, but they were taking heavy fire, and he was ordered to leave the beach. Dan said his father never found out what happened to the man: if he bled to death or if he was left to drown when the tide came in. It was a memory that haunted him.

Prior to US' involvement in World War II, President Franklin Roosevelt knew a global conflict was impending, and he had been advised that qualified medical personnel were a top priority. After having already served in World War I as an enlisted "pharmacist's mate," Thomas Kelley's father and Dan's grandfather, James Joseph Kelley, was recalled from retirement to active duty by the Navy Department in 1942. As a result, James Kelley, a retired senior chief petty officer, was commissioned as an ensign in the US Navy and reactivated for service in 1942. He was sent to the island of Guadalcanal in the Pacific Theatre where the US mounted its first major amphibious campaign of the war and where the combat was also fierce.

James Kelley was assigned as a senior medical officer for a large section of the Guadalcanal beachhead. He alone had the terrible responsibility of determining which of the badly wounded US Marines under his care had the best chance of survival. If the soldier was in decent shape, he was prepped for transport out to the white hospital ship, the *USS Rescue*, anchored offshore outside of Japanese artillery range. If Ensign Kelley determined that the marine's wounds were too severe for him to survive the journey to the ship, he quietly ordered morphine to make the dying man as comfortable as possible.

Dan said the experience was more strain than he could bear and led to his grandfather's eventual nervous breakdown.

"His sons were the same age as these men and also fighting, and it killed him," said Dan Kelley.

Guadalcanal was also where Dan Kelley's grandfather contracted the flesh-eating bacterial infection that would eventually kill him. Treatment was available, but Dan said his grandfather refused to file with Veterans Affairs as having a combat-related illness after everything he witnessed. After watching men killed in such brutal ways, he felt his suffering was minor.

He would say, "The hell with it. I'm not filing for a rash."

The war had a lifelong impact on Thomas Kelley until his death in 1988, far past the date of his final mission in April of 1945. He and his wife were living in Grand Island, New York, near Buffalo when a blizzard hit one Sunday. It was whiteout conditions, and they weren't able to see the mailbox. Thomas Kelley got up, shaved, showered, and put on a suit. His wife asked if he was nuts to consider going out. She was surprised to see her husband becoming upset. He replied, "It's Sunday, so we're going to Mass. I promised God in 1945 that, if I survived, I'd never miss Mass on a Sunday."

Dan Kelley said that his uncle felt like God did His part, so he was walking on the deal if he didn't go. It hit his wife then just how afraid Thomas must have been during the war. His uncle was a self-assured, slightly cocky guy, Dan Kelley recollected. A brilliant chemist, he was Union Carbide's "Scientist of the Year" in 1965. "He worked on everything from instant coffee to rocket fuel," Dan Kelley reflected of his uncle who would refuse to wear a tie to work, pointing to his head and saying he got paid for what was "up there," not to wear a tie. But faced with a snowstorm that prevented him from getting to church, he was in a panic. His wife ended up getting the priest on the phone as a compromise.

Thomas Kelley began his weeks-long journey to Europe from Grenier, and in his case, it wasn't a one-way trip. Dan Kelley said he was very proud of his uncle and what he and other pilots sacrificed during the war. "They stayed, knowing what they were going to face, knowing they could be the best pilot in the world and still not come back."

Kelley stated that his uncle Thomas was particularly haunted by the April 6, 1945, collision of two B-17s over the marshalling yards in Leipzig. While the accident was indeed a tragedy, additional investigation into the details also revealed an example of the surprising courage that can be shown by individuals during war. The Missing Air Crew Report of the event revealed that while five crew members did perish on the B-17 that fell into a tailspin, copilot First Lieutenant Walter Strang of P-51 numbered 43-39164 did survive along with the plane's tail gunner and navigator. The reports from the collision of the two ships are harrowing: Strang's copilot Fred Gray, who did not survive the crash, was celebrating his thirty-fifth and final mission. His final words as recalled by the surviving witnesses were, "Bombs away," and "That makes my last one." He and the rest of the crew didn't have time to remove their flak suits and jump in the seconds before the ship exploded.

Lieutenant Strang jumped with Top Turret Gunner John Randolph McCullough, as McCullough's chute was destroyed in the explosion. However, McCullough was injured and unable to hold on to his crewmate, ultimately falling to the ground and his death. Only the tail gunner from the other ship involved in the collision survived. In firm, bold handwriting, Strang recounted the horror of the event, how McCullough was trying to extricate the two of them from the plane wreckage so that the parachute they shared could be opened. Strang couldn't recall exactly when the other man let go of him, just that he witnessed his mangled body as he landed on the roof of a building, alive but surrounded by armed civilians. Strang then described being saved by a German woman and her two children who "had taken me in her house and closed the door behind an angry crowd. It was her roof that I landed on."

Of course, Thomas Kelley had no way of knowing any of this, but Strang would survive the entire ordeal and wrote in an addendum to the official report of the accident, "If the woman and children who saved my life, by arguing for my life with the angry farmers, is interrogated I would like to know the name and location. At the risk of her own life [she] pushed aside guns that were being pointed at me and helped me into her house. She fed me, tended my wounds and I therefore am forever indebted." Whether Strang ever reconnected with the woman who saved his life is unknown, as is her fate.

World War II was a vast global event, involving multiple theatres of conflict and thousands of civilians whose lives were drawn into the carnage just as surely as soldiers were. This is just one of the examples of the ripples of stories that spread outward from Grenier if you follow the thread far enough afield. Thomas Kelley was only at the base briefly, but he had a bird's eye view of history, and many of the events that he witnessed had half-lives of their own, growing and changing as they tore like flak across battlegrounds around the world.

A final example of a bomber crew that traced its point of departure back to Grenier was the 326th Bomb Squadron of the 92nd Bomb Group, which included the ball turret gunner with the infected ear that almost delayed his flight overseas, Edward McKenzie. McKenzie's crew completed the long journey through the frozen north to England where they were sent by a lorry to Podington Bomber Station 109. Despite a sign that proclaimed the newly arrived troops as "Fame's Favored Few," it quickly became clear that the 92nd was in somewhat dire straits, with orders to patch up the flak damage on anything flyable and get it back in the air. The new arrivals found many empty beds and were ominously told to take whichever one they wanted, because their former owners wouldn't need them anymore.

A few crew members, including McKenzie, ventured into London for an evening out but found it in a very different state than the bucolic setting they had left behind of Manchester, with its greenery and church steeples.

"The London air was heavy with fog and smelly with soft-coal smoke and the smoke from smoldering bomb ruins, some old and some quite new," McKenzie wrote of the excursion, which was far from the night of carousing that the men had envisioned.[67]

Monday, April 24, 1944, began with a surprise predawn wakeup call that would change McKenzie's life forever. The men were fed bacon and eggs, which made them uneasy, as it was believed that the bacon and eggs were reserved for men assigned missions they were unlikely to return from. McKenzie put a letter in the mail to his sister Doris, back home in Plaistow, New Hampshire, just in case it was his last opportunity. Inside the briefing room, the airmen were given their assignments: they would be hitting Oberpfaffenhofen, a town near Munich where the Dornier aircraft company was located. This same target had previously been reported as destroyed several times as the Allies had been unaware of how much of its infrastructure remained underground. Their mission was to take out the remaining structures.

In his account of the day written many decades later, McKenzie gave a rundown of all the materials he had with him in the turret: parachute harnesses, a Mae West life jacket, glove liners, electric gloves for the cold at high altitude, a sheepskin helmet, goggles, an oxygen mask with built-in mike and throat mike, GI shoes, a sheepskin jacket, a flak vest, and a steel helmet. The helmet was not to be worn but in case he needed to use the bathroom, possibly from fear.[68] The anxiety amongst the men was palpable, and the ball turret was a particularly difficult space to escape, given that it was too tight for McKenzie to even wear his parachute.

As the B-17 approached its target, the aircraft was surrounded by bursts of German flak. McKenzie felt the plane bounce as the bomb bay doors swung open in front of him and a payload of several tons was dropped. As their B-17, nicknamed the "Toonerville Trolley," turned towards the Munich area, it was surrounded by the Luftwaffe's Focke Wulf 190 fighter planes. Pilot Dick Anthony later described the attack that followed, as he stared directly at the flashes of gunfire coming from the wings of a German plane as they ripped through the Allied formation. Explosions followed, and their B-17 quickly lost all power on the right wing. Flames began to shoot from two of its engines.

There were two options: bail out, or try to land and ditch, hoping that they made it to the French border. Anthony determined that he would try to land. He later described the difficulty of finding an emergency landing spot amidst the hilly terrain.

"We touch ground just before reaching the brow of the hill, lose some parts, bounce up over the crest, and go sliding down the back side with no ability at all to control direction," wrote Anthony. "Only later did we see what had pulled us to the left, away from the woods and disaster which lay at the bottom of the hill. A large cherry tree was lodged in the wing, next to the cockpit."[69]

The odds that a cherry tree could stop a flaming B-17 as it careened out of the sky seem low, but photographic evidence does exist. Edward McKenzie's published report of the war included images taken by a German family that clearly show the tree lodged in the crook of the wing after the B-17 came to a halt. Written accounts by German villagers also commented on the tree, noting both the pilot's skill and the almost unbelievable luck of the crew inside the bomber.

As the dust cleared, the crew scrambled to free themselves and flee the scene.

"And now the shock of the reality hit me," McKenzie wrote. "I was alive, but on the ground deep in the heart of Nazi Germany, and would not be going back to my base, nor to my home in New Hampshire, probably ever again."

McKenzie and the other crew members darted for the cover of the tree line as German villagers began to appear on the horizon. When he found himself surrounded, he threw up his arms and shouted, "*Kamerad*," one of the few German words he knew, learned from dime novels about downed World War I flying aces. It translates to "comrade."

The captured Americans were eventually moved into a stone barn where they were told to remove their clothes and write down their names and ranks. After that, the exhausted crew members were ordered into a car and driven off to the next stage of their wartime journey: imprisonment at Stalag Seventeen.

Official U.S. Army Air Corps photo of Jean D. Grenier.
Courtesy of the Manchester (N.H.) Historic Association

And 'Babs' Keith of Grenier Field Never Took a Lesson

—Official Photo, U. S. Army Air Forces

A 19-year-old Derry girl who never took an art lesson in her life is attracting considerable attention with her "Petty" drawings in the Grenier Field Beacon, the weekly paper published for servicemen and civilian personnel at the local air base. She is Miss Barbara "Babs" Keith, pictured above. Below is the latest piece of her work. Miss Keith also writes the jingle which appears with each drawing.

Barbara "Babs" Keith and one of her creations

A view of Grenier Air Base, undated.
Aviation Museum of N.H. archives, Ed Brouder

The 1960 Civil Air Patrol Tri-state Encampment.
Photo courtesy Carl Stidsen

Former Grenier CAP cadet Carl Stidsen at a missile site in 1968.
Photo courtesy Carl Stidsen

The firing range at Grenier in the 1950s.
Aviation Museum of N.H. archives, courtesy Ed McKenzie

Sgt. Robert Dinan of Nashua takes a cup of milk from a Red Cross worker.
Dinan was one of a wave of 535 airmen
who returned to Grenier at the end of World War II."

Air evacuees who landed at Grenier and Pat Purrington, a WAC on the base.
From the Beacon, Sept. 8, 1945

Images of a much quieter Grenier
in the winter of 1967, after the military had vacated the field.

A photo of Irene Keith filling up a P-51 Mustang in 1944

Edward McKenzie (middle) in 1951 after returning from his time as a prisoner of war overseas.
Aviation Museum of N.H. archives, Ed McKenzie

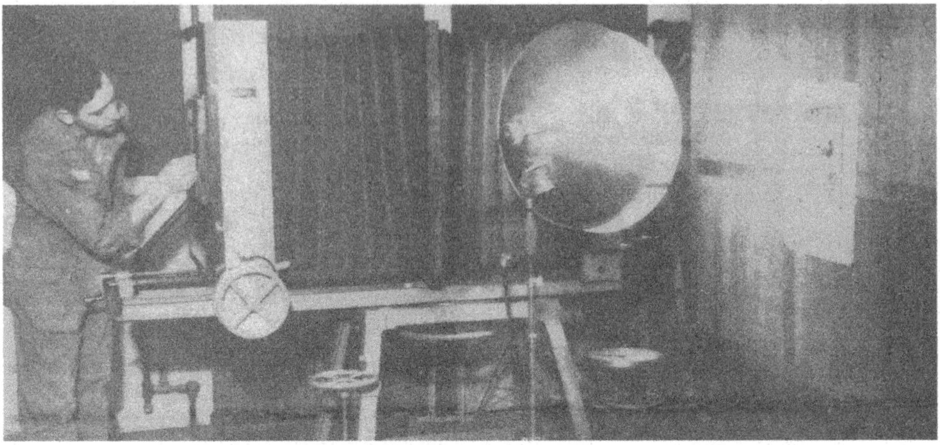

An image of the base newspaper, the Beacon, being made.
From the Beacon, April 10, 1943

2nd Lt. Allman Culbertson from Danville, N.Y., surrounded by his cousins at the Manchester Airport in 1939.
Courtesy Genevieve Stannard Rowell

A Civil Air Patrol training session, including a very young participant.
Courtesy Paul Kelly

Sen. Joseph McCarthy of Wisconsin disembarking at Grenier

An edition of the Manchester Union Leader demonstrates the fast progress at Grenier

UNIQUE 'O. P.'

July 16, 1942 Thursday

"Somewhere in New Hampshire" this house boat is now being used as an observation post for the Aircraft Warning Service. It is believed to be the first post in the country located on a houseboat. Equipped with modern conveniences, the "O.P." is manned 24 hours a day. July 16, 1942

A New Hampshire houseboat that became an observation post during the war.
Aviation Museum of N.H. archives

A caravan of WACs entering the base

Officials survey the scene of the explosion in Bedford (N.H.) in July, 1944.
From the Beacon

An image of the building that now houses the Aviation Museum of N.H.

LOUNGE. Officer's club displaying everyone's favourite pin-up girl.

An image of a lounge for American servicemen at a base in Britain.
Source: A Red Cross booklet produced for the 388th Bomb Group (H)

One of many crashes near Grenier Air Base in the 1940s

Sisters Ruth Mattingly (right) and Vicki Dyes (left).
Photo courtesy Cathy Hawkins

AIR BASE NURSES TEST GAS MASKS

Emerging from a heavy smoke screen laid down Tuesday at the Manchester Air Base, three army nurses are pictured above getting used to gas masks as part of the base gas drill program. The smoke screen was laid down by the base Chemical Co. in the first smoke drill held in Manchester. Nurses include Gladys Lees of Milford, Catherine Gura of Southington, Conn., and Harriet Boyle of Manchester. (Other photos, Page 12.)

Army nurses at Grenier test gas masks.

Source: Grenier scrapbook at the Manchester Historic Association

Manchester

AIR BASE SEEN AS TOPS IN NATION

Night Duty

Fire Call

Base Commander

Preparation

Pets

Hospitalization

Boston American article proclaiming Grenier "Tops in the Nation"

Grenier Air Base Main Post Exchange, undated.
Aviation Museum of N.H. archives, Ed Brouder

Army nurses serving at Grenier Air Base.
Source: Grenier scrapbook, Manchester Historic Association

CHAPTER 4

"OUR SAFETY PROBLEM": THREATS ON THE HOME FRONT

WHILE THOUSANDS OF AIRMEN WERE LEAVING Grenier during the height of the war years to face danger, death, and imprisonment, a few foreign prisoners of war were also coming into New England. In October of 1944, Edward DeKostic, father of Rick DeKostic from Merrimack, New Hampshire, landed at Grenier Field in a B-24 Liberator. Ed, the aircraft bombardier, and his fellow crewmembers were headed for the European theater. Like hundreds of other crews, Grenier was their final US stop before flying on to Gander, Newfoundland.

According to the combined wartime memories shared with Rick by his dad, the pilot, Carl Gigowski, and the nose gunner, Herb Little, whom Rick met in 1992, their visit to Grenier was not a pleasant experience.

"Apparently they were scheduled to have a brief layover of only about [twenty-four] hours, but bad weather turned their stay into a week," Rick DeKostic wrote via email. "It was cold, rainy, and as a crew heading overseas, they were confined to the base without much to do. Additionally, there was a threat of sabotage to aircraft on the field, so the crew was required to guard their B-24, day and night!

"Herb Little told me that my father had acquired a carbine, which he stored in the plane's nose, near his position. I can imagine Dad now, sleeping on the Liberator's floor, next to his rifle or a sidearm, and trying to stay warm, like his fellow crewmates. After seven days of this, they'd had enough of Grenier and left for Gander, Newfoundland. A few months later, however, they may have wished they were back at Grenier . . ."

Edward DeKostic and the other members of the crew went on to complete some thirty-five combat missions with the 15th Air Force, serving under the 485th Bomb Group, 828th Bomb Squadron. Rick DeKostic was unsure of why the crew was required to keep such a close eye on the plane for sabotage; his father had died seven years before he met the other crew members in 1992.

"If I asked, and any of them told me, I don't recall what they said; unfortunately, Carl's diary doesn't indicate why they had to guard the plane either."

The extra layer of vigilance may have had something to do with a man named Franz Bacher, a twenty-eight-year-old German prisoner of war who was on the run from US authorities. During World War II, New England maintained over a dozen prison camps, with one of them located in the state of New Hampshire, known as Camp Stark. About 250 German and Austrian soldiers, most of whom were captured in North Africa, lived in Camp Stark while working in the surrounding forest where they cut pulpwood vital to wartime industry. A Berlin, New Hampshire, paper firm called Brown Company was understaffed owing to the war, and German POWs were the solution to helping meet the company's wartime quota.

The prisoners were transferred up to the camp, which was located only thirty miles south of the Canadian border, from Fort Devens, Massachusetts, not Grenier. However, Camp Stark was not known for its security, and Franz Bacher managed to escape into the New Hampshire woods in August of 1944 while chopping trees. He wouldn't be apprehended until October, the same month and year that Ed DeKostic flew into Grenier. Bacher was a political prisoner in Nazi Germany before being sent to North Africa to fight. He was an Austrian leftist who spoke four languages, hated military life, and wrote in a note that he was fleeing Camp Stark in order to pursue art, which he did. After leaving Camp Stark, he walked to Springfield, New Hampshire, and got on a bus to New York City where he sold paintings and slept in Central Park. He was apprehended at an art supply store in Union Square on October 14, 1944.[70] It would make sense if the command at Grenier kept a wary eye out for any potential sightings of the German POW who escaped from a camp in the same state, even if the man was more interested in making art than waging war.

Winston McCarty of the Tilton Veterans Home, who grew up near Stark in West Milan, New Hampshire, can remember the camp when it was operational during the war.

"There was a big open wire fence around the compound," he said. "People would drive by, and you could look in and see prisoners wandering around to pass the time."

Cars weren't supposed to stop and peek in, but he said that everyone did it anyway.

There were several threats to the civilian population on the home front of the eastern US during the years of World War II. There was the fear of fire-bombing and enemy aircraft or the sabotage and theft of US military aircraft from a base, but there was also the looming threat of what could come out of the Atlantic. About an hour to the east of Grenier, Portsmouth Naval Shipyard saw its own boom during the war years, breaking records for the highest number of submarines produced in a single year.[71] Shortly after Pearl Harbor, an active minefield was laid at the entrance to Portsmouth Harbor. This, along with a submarine net, were intended to protect Portsmouth from German submarines.[72]

The *Boston Herald* wrote of the proximity between Grenier and the coast: "Fort-five miles away, as the bomber flies, is salt water at Portsmouth—and Portsmouth Navy Yard may some day be glad that Manchester is an air base."[73] Due in part to this proximity, Grenier served for some time as the operating base for airborne submarine patrol units such as the 13th anti-sub group in 1942 and 1943.

Henry Jack Kornegay, Jr., was one of the soldiers who went through anti-submarine training. He was studying at the University of Mississippi before the war broke out and, like many pilots of the day, had never flown in a plane before he entered the military. He went over to the recruiting station with a college friend and didn't even intend to apply to join the military at the time; he was just accompanying the classmate who was signing up. But then the flight surgeon came over and asked him to strip for the physical exam, and he decided to sign up anyway on the spot.[74]

Kornegay wound up at Maxwell Field, Alabama, for training and then on to Avon Park, Florida, for primary flight training. He finished flight training in the days just before Pearl Harbor. In a recorded interview, he recalled the day after his graduation party from Basic, out with a few other couples looking for alligators on a date night when they heard about Pearl Harbor on the car radio. After being sent to multi-engine training at Turner Field, Kornegay's next stop was Grenier where he was checked out in a B-18. By 1942, Douglas B-18 Bolos were being phased out as the Army Air Corps' standard bomber and used more frequently in anti-submarine warfare.[75] This was exactly what Kornegay was assigned to, flying on anti-submarine patrols along the East Coast until sometime in 1943.

Kornegay would eventually be transferred to overseas combat in England as part of the Eighth Air Force. It's unclear from the filmed interview of his experience, but perhaps this is because the Battle of the Atlantic reached its peak in early 1943 as the Allies managed to sink nearly a hundred German U-boats in the first five months of the year, significantly affecting Germany's ability to menace Allied shipping. The threat of German U-boats off America's shores had been a serious one very close to home for the earlier part the war. When the German U-boats arrived off the East Coast, they found unprotected shipping lanes with unescorted vessels, fully lighted and starkly silhouetted by city lights. They would remain submerged during the day and come to the surface at night.[76]

In a campaign known to the Germans as "The American Shooting Season," the U-boats "enjoyed for a time a veritable Eldorado, and their successes rose to undreamed-of figures . . . Targets were so plentiful that it was more often lack of torpedoes than shortage of fuel which compelled the U-boats to turn for home."[77] In total, German submarines sank about five thousand Allied ships throughout the course of the war.[78]

Another Grenier-based soldier, Captain Pete C. Sianis, was awarded an Air Medal for serving over two hundred hours on anti-submarine patrol. The citation commended his efforts under "trying conditions such as restricted visibility, low ceilings and icing conditions encountered on the large number of flights necessary to perform this hazardous patrol of great responsibility. Possibility of encountering enemy ships of fighter type or anti-aircraft fire added to the hazards of these missions."[79]

U-boats were not the only danger to servicemen that lurked close to home. Training accidents were a major source of casualties during the war. Pilot carelessness, poor component design, inadequate training, carelessness of others, bad weather, improper maintenance, and sometimes pure bad luck claimed thousands of lives outside of combat.[80] Aircraft production more than doubled in the US the year after the nation entered World War II. Aircraft factories produced more than 48,000 aircraft in 1942, which went up to 96,318 by 1944. As new pilots were sent out, accidents increased as well. In 1941, there were 233 fatal AAF accidents, which increased to 1,108, resulting in 2,395 deaths, 277 injuries, and loss of over 1,200 aircraft. In 1942, AAF commanders addressed safety issues internally in a classified memo titled "Our Safety Problem."

By 1943, there were six fatal training accidents per day. There were over 6,350 fatal aircraft accidents across the continental US during World War II, resulting in 7,114 lost aircraft and the deaths of 15,530 pilots, crew members, and bystanders on the ground. The highest number were killed during advanced training. The Army Air Corps lost over 4,500 servicemembers in actual combat against Japanese armed forces, but 7,100 lives were lost in training accidents in the US.[81]

One of the deadliest of these accidents in the Manchester area took place on Monday morning, April 24, 1944, when a group of ten Air Force men boarded a B-24 Liberator at Grenier in instrument conditions. The ceiling was low at only thirteen hundred feet, and the mood must have been somber as the men were leaving the base for the first leg of their journey into combat by way of Goose Bay, Labrador. It being April in New Hampshire, the trees were likely still bare, with the early fuzz of new leaves, the weather pivoting between the final lingering tendrils of winter and spring with intermittent fog and rain.

Whether the crew was fearful of the war they were about to fly into or if they were eager to serve and fight, we'll never know, as within about ten minutes, something went horribly wrong. In the usually quiet town of Epsom, New Hampshire, a large explosion tore through the air, followed by a series of smaller blasts. Joseph Bozek, a twenty-five-year-old resident of Mountain Road, said he heard the initial explosion and ran a mile or two through the woods, directed by the sounds of smaller ongoing explosions. Bozek had hoped to offer aid to any survivors of the plane crash but found none. The B-24 had cut a swath of about three hundred yards across the mountain, leaving a path of wreckage and the bodies of crew members.

Grenier personnel in command cars and ambulances arrived at the scene around noon, unable to do much on roads described as "a quagmire" with an emergency scene that soon drew a host of curious onlookers to the muddy country byways. Of the crew, only nine bodies were initially recovered, with military personnel continuing their search for the tenth man all through the night, using a makeshift road built by a Civil Air Patrol group amidst rain and fog in dense brush. The last of the missing airmen's bodies was finally recovered beneath the wrecked fuselage.

Burial rites were held on April 26, 1944, at the Grenier Field Chapel. The ten men were all in their twenties, save for Flight Engineer Sergeant Francis M. Weaver, who was thirty-six, married, and employed by the Humble Pipeline Company back home in Bryan, Texas. The crew also counted twenty-five-year-old Lloyd Utley, a salesclerk from Indiana who held only a grammar school education. Brooklyn-born Second Lieutenant William George Hunold had been in the military for three years by that April, having enlisted at the age of twenty with the occupation of "student." If you find Lloyd's casualty record, his death is described as "DNB," short for "Died Non-Battle."

The remaining dead were identified as Second Lieutenant Marvin M. Rupp, twenty-six, of Winfield, Kansas (pilot); Second Lieutenant James H. Jones, twenty-one, of Alumbank, Pennsylvania (copilot); Second Lieutenant Ardeth K. Gannon, twenty-six, of Rockwell City, Iowa (navigator); Staff Sergeant Anthony L. Ferrone, twenty-seven, of New York, New York (radio operator); Staff Sergeant Marion L. Wolfgang, twenty-three, of Illinois (flight engineer); Sergeant John L. Eddins, twenty-six, of Kingsville, Texas (gunner); Sergeant Joseph H. Negele, twenty-three, of Newark, Ohio (radio operator).

Investigators would later comment that the ship likely exploded immediately upon impact with the rock face of the mountain top. The wreckage was in such a state of destruction, it was difficult to conduct a thorough examination of the accident's cause, but investigators hypothesized that Rupp was struggling in the cloud layer and lowered the ship in an attempt to fly by contact, using visible landmarks or points of reference.

Accounts of the crash in Epsom from the 1940s provide differing answers on the name of the mountain where the accident took place: there's Washtub Mountain, Mount Delight, and Fort Mountain. However, the majority of reports called the spot where the tragedy occurred "Fort Mountain," and one or two acknowledged that Washtub Mountain was a former or casual name for Fort Mountain. The area of the crash is still rural in the twenty-first century. An access road goes up to Fort Mountain, which at fourteen hundred feet seems more like a big hill than a mountain. The area is surrounded by dense woodlands, fields, and logging areas. Mountain Road feels like a lonely place, especially on a drab day in early spring, when any vehicle driving along it stands out. It's easy to visualize the difficulty of conducting a large-scale recovery mission in the area, hauling wreckage and remains down the muddy slope of Fort Mountain.

There are a number of wreck sites in New Hampshire that are memorialized by a plaque of some kind: the B-52 that went down in a swamp in Fremont, for example, or the B-18 that still lies in pieces on Mount Waternomee following a crash in 1942 after departing Westover Field in Chicopee, Massachusetts. Fort Mountain doesn't appear to have any visible wounds left behind from the wreck that took ten lives nor any obvious markers of the event. Perhaps it was because, at this point of the war, the news was filled with continuous accounts of death. A scan of the headlines from that week includes lives frequently lost on bombing campaigns. Even in quiet New Hampshire, the news marched steadily on after the dead were buried.

The accidents that took place around Grenier Air Base stimulated the curiosity of many local residents, including those too young to enlist themselves. Scott Guilbert can remember stories from his father, Roland Guilbert, of growing up around Grenier and avidly watching its activities. An amateur photographer and aviation enthusiast, Roland would count the dozens of B-17s, B-24s, and P-51 Mustangs that flew in, once tallying fifty P-51s in a day. One day, Roland and a friend were outside when they saw a P-51 engaged in a mock dogfight. They were puzzled by why it was flying so low, and then they heard a thud. The young men went to investigate and found a still-smoldering crash site near Bartley Hill Road in Londonderry surrounded by Jeeps, ambulances, and trucks from the base.

The two teenagers watched from the woods, trying to get a glimpse of what was going on, but Roland knelt on a stick that snapped in two. In the blink of an eye, he found himself surrounded by military police and ushered into a vehicle that would take him straight back home with a reprimand. Months later he would discreetly venture back to the site and discover a buckle and buttons from the pilot's uniform, which he turned in to the base headquarters, soliciting groans and rolled eyes.

"You've opened a whole can of worms," he was told by military personnel who were not looking forward to trekking back out to the site of the plane crash to review all over again whether anything of value was left behind.

Scott Guilbert tells another family story of an uncle who was stationed in Bermuda and encountered an anti-submarine patrol on a refueling stop there.

When he asked where they were headed next with their B-17 and was told Grenier, he was surprised by the coincidence and wanted to hop a ride as his fiancé lived in Londonderry. The fact that Scott's uncle was unsuccessful in his endeavor to hitch a ride home proved to be very fortunate, as the plane clipped the trees near Saint Jude Parish in Londonderry and went down. Scott's dad, Roland, once again snuck a peak through the woods, but he wasn't the only local kid to do so. One boy who lived in the neighborhood found a funny-looking piece of equipment in the rubble and decided to take it home.

As it turned out, the boy's new toy wasn't just any piece of junk lost in the wreck: it was a Norden bombsight, one of the most valued and heavily protected pieces of technology in World War II. The Norden, along with the Sperry bombsight, were developed in the years leading up to World War II to allow for greater accuracy from the air, especially at higher altitudes. The Norden integrated readings of air and wind speed, wind direction, and angle of drift, all while adjusting for these factors automatically to release the bomb at just the right moment. A Norden was installed on the Enola Gay, the B-29 that would later drop the atomic bomb on Hiroshima.

The bombsight was a piece of technology capable of changing aerial warfare, but a lot rested on the skills of the bombardiers who were charged with programming them. Since Grenier was the final stop before flying overseas for many soldiers, some crews received technical training on the bombsight at Grenier with a simulator in building T-824 on the southwest side of the field. When not in use for training, the bombsights at Grenier were guarded under lock and key. The secrecy of this invention was taken so seriously, the crew was ordered to destroy the bombsight in the event of the plane going down to keep it from enemy hands.[82]

Robert Doucette of Manchester, New Hampshire, confirmed that his father, a bombardier in the Eighth Air Force, did in fact destroy the Norden on his own ship when it went down over German-held France, but he wasn't certain if the destruction occurred before the aircraft hit the ground or after. It couldn't have been an easy feat while hurtling towards Earth. Since the B-17 from Bermuda went down quickly, clearly this didn't happen in the chaos that ensued. Military police quickly began canvassing the area for anyone who knew the whereabouts of the bombsight.

"The MPs went looking for it, found out that 'Johnny' has it, knocked on the door and the kid's mother came out," Scott Guilbert explained. "'Oh, you mean this thing?' says the mom. So the little kid lost his souvenir."

In a separate incident, a resident near the crossroads of Routes 28 and 128 in Londonderry saw a P-38 come streaking down from the sky and called the fire department, certain that he had witnessed a horrible crash. He ran towards where he'd last seen the plane and came upon the pilot sitting completely still in the cockpit, his head down. The man thought for sure that he was approaching a corpse, but upon drawing closer, it became clear that the man was very intently filling out his logbook and had managed a lucky emergency landing.

It wasn't just aircraft training accidents that those who lived in proximity to Grenier had to contend with, however.

There were other forms of crimes and accidents on the base. In October of 1943, a Boston and Maine train crashed into an Army vehicle, killing thirty-year-old Private Clyde Williamson and injuring four other soldiers.[83] One headline out of Enfield, New Hampshire, in 1944 read, "Veteran Pacific Flier Finds Enfield More Dangerous," and detailed how an Air Corps sergeant spent thirty-two months dodging Japanese bombs and shells only to be lit on fire after two days on furlough when he and his brother were attempting to start a car and a backfire caused a can of gasoline to combust, badly burning his left arm, leg, and hand.

The first person to die on Grenier Air Base from any cause was a soldier named Private Harold J. Kieva, twenty-two, who was found on August 5, 1941, with his throat slashed in a barracks shower, a razor located on the floor nearby. Unofficial reports noted that Kieva had been despondent since enlisting and being assigned to the 45th Bombardment Group (which dealt with anti-submarine patrols at the time). An official probe would later conclude that the cause of death was, in fact, suicide.[84]

"Military regulations require no report to civil authorities in the case of a serviceman's death," it was explained at the base headquarters at the time of Kieva's suicide. In this instance, the Manchester Police Department was notified and called to the scene; however, it's less clear if this was done in later incidents.

A spate of accidents occurred in the guard huts around the base, usually because of carelessness with a weapon. One such death occurred on the base in 1941 when Private Peter Colon, twenty-one, of New York City was shot and killed instantly early in the morning while on guard duty. Private Harold L. Tocas, a fellow guard and close friend of the victim, was inspecting his weapon prior to the changing of shift when it went off accidentally. The bullet hit Tocas, who was a member of the 34th Squadron of the 33rd Air Base Group, in the back of the head. The shooter was held in custody pending the findings of a military court.[85] Tocas (alternately spelled Tokas by some newspapers) would ultimately be charged with manslaughter, but it's unclear what happened from there.[86]

In another mirror instance on the cold morning of January 31, 1942, a twenty-three-year-old Finnish-American private named Reino Marttila was rushed to the hospital on Grenier Air Base with a gunshot wound.[87] Hospital records indicate that the wound was cervical (to the neck region of the backbone), and news coverage of the time indicated that the shooting was an accident by Marttila's fellow guard, Corporal Robert D. Osborne. Despite an attempted blood transfusion, Marttila did not survive his injury.

An investigation was conducted on the incident, with the findings presented to a military court, but the results remain elusive. A request for information to the National Personnel Records Center confirmed that nothing about the incident could be located and that, if documents concerning the shooting of Marttila did exist, they would have been in the area of the records facility burned by the 1973 fire.

Yet another shooting of a guard took place the same month that Marttila died, when a Black soldier was shot through the body by a .30 caliber rifle slug. Both Private David Gerard and Private Ross Moore were in a warming hut when Moore's rifle discharged. Gerard's back was to the other soldier at the time. Moore would later claim that he was loading the gun when the shot went off. The bullet went through Gerard's lung and out his upper right chest, then continued its trajectory, breaking the window of the guard hut and landing in the snow outside. Fortunately, Gerard did survive this accident and was able to get help from civilians by running to a nearby gas station, yelling that he had been shot. Although newspapers of the day reported that preliminary findings indicated this was also an accidental shooting, it's difficult to truly understand the circumstances without the ability to review the final judgment of the military investigation.[88] Without additional information, some questions remain. Why did Gerard have to run to a gas station for help? Perhaps in the chaos of the moment, the injured man tried to get away from the scene as quickly as he could, but shouldn't Moore have been the one to seek out aid if he had fired the shot by accident?

It's one of the many stories from Grenier that lacks a satisfactory conclusion, and any speculation is just that without solid backup. The accidents, shootings, and suicide are examples of how time can swallow even the most traumatic events and how danger could lurk on a base, even on the home front.

The actual cause of Private Gerard's shooting may be nebulous, but there certainly were tensions on the base between troops of different backgrounds and from different regions of the country. In June of 1941, President Roosevelt issued Executive Order 8802 banning discriminatory employment practices by federal agencies and all unions and companies engaged in war-related work. However, this mainly pertained to defense positions. Segregation in the armed forces persisted (including on Grenier Air Base) until Executive Order 9981 was signed by President Harry S. Truman in 1948.

In *Half American: The Epic Story of African Americans Fighting World War II at Home and Abroad*, Dartmouth professor Matthew F. Delmont invites readers to reflect on long-held notions about the valor of World War II from a US standpoint and the hypocrisy of fighting Nazism while holding rigidly to segregated structures at home.

"While many Americans hold idealized notions of World War II as a 'good war' fought by the Greatest Generation—an era when America was supposedly greater than it is today—the experiences of Black Americans tell a different story."[89]

This is not a topic that can be summarized in a few short paragraphs. For a more complete understanding of the politics, history, and experiences of Black Americans during World War II, Delmont's book provides in-depth context. But a notable moment in the fight for equality on the home front came when the *Pittsburgh Courier* published a letter by twenty-six-year-old James G. Thompson, a defense worker who was confined to working in the cafeteria of the aircraft manufacturing company where he was employed.

Thompson's letter, "Should I Sacrifice to live 'Half American'?" challenged the lofty idealism of the war effort and invoked the "V for Victory" sign being used to signify triumph over Axis aggression. A double V would symbolize two victories: one against foreign enemies, and one against the oppression at home.

During World War II, 2.5 million African American men registered for the draft, with over a million inducted into the armed forces. In addition to thousands of Black women, these inductees served in all branches of service and in all Theaters of Operation during the war despite facing opposition by the factions of the military and government to keep them out of the armed services. The *Pittsburgh Courier*, once the country's most widely circulated Black newspaper, reported that Army officials ordered draft boards in New England to exclude Black Americans in the first draft of the war.[90]

On Grenier, most soldiers of color were assigned to the 37th Aviation Squadron. In addition to serving as firemen, cooks, clerks, mechanics, orderlies, and other jobs, many of them were guards, in charge of any prisoners on the base.

Black troops on Grenier lived in a separate barracks known informally as "The Village," described by author and historian Ed Brouder as being located on the east side of Access Road behind the homes of Ernest and Ruth Smith and Henry and Beatrice Jacques. A search through the woods near the side of the road in that area today reveals several concrete foundations, visible through the overgrowth and the trees.

By September 1942, there were eight hundred Black soldiers stationed at Grenier Base in Manchester, according to local writer and historian Aurore Eaton. Segregation infiltrated soldiers' social lives outside of their official duties as well; with the growth of the USO in Manchester, a separate recreation building on the base that doubled as a dance hall was designated for use by the Black soldiers on Grenier Base. In early January 1943, Margaret Dallas, a young Black woman from Salt Lake City, Utah, was hired as the on base USO hostess.

The Aviation Squadron column in the *Beacon* often mentions soldiers' exploits away from Manchester in "Bean Town." In a 2006 interview by Aurore Eaton, Manchester resident Faye L'Ecuyer recalled an episode on the dance floor at a USO function:

"Once, you know, at the USO . . . it wasn't a big band night or anything, but they were dancing on the floor, two young, really young, black men. They were soldiers. They had these beautiful women with them . . . One by one, stopped dancing just because, that's a shame, I thought that was terrible. They stopped dancing, because, they didn't want to dance with the black men. I didn't think it was right . . . They, they're fighting for our country, they're going to get killed just like our white boys, you know."[91]

While some members of the community, like L'Ecuyer, were accepting of the Black soldiers, their presence represented a change in Manchester that not everyone was happy about. One incident reported in the *Union Leader* in 1943 tells of a brawl that ensued when White soldiers tried to order Black soldiers out of a Bridge Street café. Military leaders on the base were reluctant to comment on the episode in the paper.

Tensions could run high at the Village barracks as well where quarters were close. Private John Jackson of Macomb, Mississippi, was shot in the chest and killed instantly by Captain John Coker when an argument about turning off the lights escalated.

Military commanders questioned the competency and "aggressiveness" of Black troops, which resulted in inconsistent training. Training was often less thorough in general because it was believed Black troops would never actually see battle. In instances where that turned out to be a false assumption, it could lead to deadly consequences. This was exactly what happened in the case of the 366th Infantry Regiment, which was attached to the 92nd Infantry Division.

One of only four US regiments with all Black officers at the platoon level, many of the members of the 366th were African American, but others were individuals with dark skin from other ethnicities. Active in both World Wars, the 366th was responsible for guarding bridges, railroad trestles, and Air Force bases across New England from Cape Cod to Canada. This likely explains why newspaper coverage in the *Union Leader* indicates they were in Manchester for at least a brief period despite being stationed for about two years at Fort Devens.

When the 366th was initially sent to Italy in 1944, they were assigned to guard duties. The division commander of the 92nd, Major General Edward Almond, was known for opposing equal treatment of Black Americans in the service until the day he died. He notoriously told the 366th upon their arrival overseas, "I did not send for you. Your Negro newspapers, Negro politicians and white friends have insisted on you seeing combat and I shall see that you get combat and your share of casualties." When finally sent to the front months later, pleas for additional training were ignored, and they were instead divided into smaller units. The regiment suffered thirteen hundred casualties, one-third of their group, after fighting ferociously on the Gothic Line, the final heavily fortified main German defensive line in northern Italy.

The troops returned home to more unequal treatment. When soldiers from the 366th arrived back on US soil at the war's end, they were loaded onto buses and ordered to the back because the seats in front were reserved for White German POWs.[92] The 366th rose to the challenge of this domestic combat with tenacity. At the urging of friends from his former Army unit, Edward W. Brooke interrupted his law career to run for the Massachusetts House of Representatives in 1950. He won his race, becoming the first Black politician from Massachusetts to serve in Congress. When Brooke was elected to the US Senate in 1966, he became the first popularly elected Black senator. Later, Brooke became the first senator to publicly call for President Nixon's resignation.

"In every regard, we were treated as second-class soldiers, if not worse, and we were angry," Brooke recalled of his military service later in life. "I felt a personal frustration and bitterness I had not known before in my life."[93]

Imagine being a resident of Manchester in July of 1944. It's the night before Independence Day, and since the war began, you've been primed to watch for the slightest suspicious thing: any unidentified aircraft in the skies, strangers behaving oddly, the smallest detail that could be the first indication of an invasion on US soil. Maybe you've glimpsed the silhouettes of German subs surfacing just off the coast. Now, imagine that, as you prepare for July 4, you hear an enormous explosion ring out from the area near Grenier Air Base, shattering windows as far as fifty miles away and cracking walls in Nashua.[94]

It's not difficult to understand why residents of Manchester thought the base was being bombed, especially since police weren't able to reach the scene for some time owing to the chaos that ensued after the explosion. Grenier Air Base came alive that night as everyone in the area raced to understand the cause of the blast. The *Beacon* printed later that week, "When the explosion went off Monday night, Pvt. Elsie Walker got up and put her dog tags on."[95] An *AP* article reported "thousands of people milling through the streets of the city, running wildly on foot and on autos."

A *Beacon* article titled "Grenierites Interpret Blast Differently" recorded some of the reactions around the base in the wake of the blast. A *Beacon* staff writer was sipping a scotch when the explosion rattled the Venetian blinds. The steward of the building came running into the room, announcing his thoughts that it was the switch on the oil heater, because "it makes a little 'poof' like that." Another private speculated that a carbon dioxide tank truck had gone up, and still another (very reasonably) thought the sound came from a B-24 crashing.[96]

The explosion turned out to have taken place at John B. Bedrick Hardware Company in neighboring Bedford, New Hampshire, where only a crater was left behind where two powder houses once stood. Miraculously, no one was killed and only a minor injury reported, but the incident shows just how on edge the community was even as the end of the war was finally beginning to come into sight.

CHAPTER 5

A RETURN TO ABNORMAL: DAWN OF THE ATOMIC AGE

BY 1944, THE TIDE OF THE WAR WAS BEGINNING TO shift. The Allies had come a long way from the beginning of World War II when victory was far from a guarantee and, to many Americans, the conflict seemed far away. Many families had lost sons to the fighting, and almost everyone had tightened their belts, giving up everyday goods and offering whatever services they could to the Allied cause, regardless of their military status. By the end of the war, the comparatively small state of New Hampshire had lost 1,203 service members; more densely populated Massachusetts lost over 10,000.[97] Chances were high that, by its end, the average person in New England knew at least someone affected directly by the war. World leaders were desperate to put an end to the conflict by any means necessary. To General of the Army Dwight Eisenhower, that meant retaking France in what would become known as the largest amphibious invasion in military history: Operation Overlord.

Eisenhower's "Order of the Day" statement issued to troops before the invasion of Normandy on June 6, 1944, reminded them of the progress of the last few years, giving credit to Allied pilots and air crews:

"Much has happened since the Nazi triumphs of 1940–41. The United Nations have inflicted upon the Germans great defeats, in open battle, man-to-man. Our air offensive has seriously reduced their strength in the air and their capacity to wage war on the ground."[98]

Almost 133,000 troops from the US, the British Commonwealth, and their allies landed on D-Day, marking the largest amphibious assault in history. From a distance, New Hampshire and Grenier Air Base played a role in the assault as a final training point for the Eighth Air Force troops.

The invasion wasn't planned overnight. Almost immediately after Pearl Harbor, Allied forces concluded that liberating Europe from the influence of Nazi Germany was a priority over the conflict in the Pacific. However, breaking through German defenses would certainly be extremely bloody. The Allies spent years preparing for D-Day, opting to gather experience in North Africa and Sicily before launching the attack.

As early as 1942, the BBC launched a fake appeal for photographs and postcards from across the coasts of Europe. In reality, it was a way to gather intelligence. The millions of photos that were sent in helped military commanders to establish the best potential landing points for an invasion, which is how the beaches in Normandy were selected.[99] The beaches were chosen for a few reasons: they lay within range of air cover and were less heavily defended than the Pas de Calais, the shortest distance between Great Britain and the continent.

The US plotted to deceive the Germans into believing Pas de Calais would be the site of the invasion. Eisenhower's staff created a mythical 1st US Army Group under General George S. Patton and saw to it that known enemy agents received information on the status of Patton's force. Much of the planning in the days and weeks leading up to D-Day revolved around the weather forecast. D-Day was planned for May 31 and moved, with two periods in the following month identified as suitable, on the basis of tides and the amount of moonlight: June 5–7 and June 18–20. German Commander Erwin Rommel famously went to celebrate his wife's birthday in Germany on June 6, believing the weather to be too poor for the invasion to begin.[100]

The Allied invasion stretched across five beaches codenamed "Utah," "Omaha," "Gold," "Juno," and "Sword." The plan was for heavy aerial bombing to take out Nazi gun positions and destroy key roads and bridges, cutting off Germany's retreat as well as reinforcements. Then paratroopers would drop in to secure inland positions before the mass amphibious landing of 150,000 infantrymen from Britain, Canada, and the US, who would quickly overwhelm the crippled Nazi defenses. Eight-hundred and sixty-two heavy bombers were dispatched in the operation. Fighter support was provided by 365 aircraft, including 175 P-47s, 46 P-38s, and 144 P-51s.[101]

Among the air combatants that day were two brothers who had recently trained at Grenier: Edward M. Rex and John Leo Rex. The Rex brothers had both graduated from Turner Field and were assigned to Grenier Air Base where they flew A-20 Havoc bombers. Both brothers became B-24s pilots assigned to the 486th Bomb Group, 833rd Bomb Squadron based at Sudbury, England. On the day of the D-Day invasion, Edward was assigned to his brother John's crew as a command pilot. He sat opposite John, maintained radio contact with the group leader, and checked the squadron's position in the group. John was assigned to lead the top squadron of the 486th Bomb Group during the invasion.[102]

Much later in life, John reflected back on the lead-up to the D-Day invasion as tension built prior to one of the most consequential battles of the war:

"Assignments for the following day missions were posted in the Orderly Room on the night before the mission. When we looked at the schedule for June 6, 1944, there was nothing unusual about the crew assignments except in the case of my crew . . . It was a 2:00 a.m. wake-up call that suggested to us that it might be a long mission.

"Upon arriving at the briefing room, we noticed an abundance of high-ranking officers present. Among them was General Frederick Castle, commanding general of the Second Air Division, Eighth Air Force.

"When we were all seated and the meeting was called to attention, the briefing officer pulled away the curtain which covered the activity map. There on the map was the shortest mission flight we ever experienced. The route tape went from our base in East England to a French town named Caen. It was at this time that General Castle was introduced, and he very seriously informed us that this was *the* D-Day mission. He told us that our group (486th Bomb Group) would be the first Eighth Air Force group over the invasion beaches and that our target was Caen, an important rail supply for the Germans.

"He then asked Ed and I if we had any objections to flying together in the High Squadron lead aircraft. (Soon after D-Day, the Air Force issued regulations not allowing blood relatives to fly in the same aircraft.)

"We were scheduled to be over the target (Caen) at H-Hour minus thirty. H-Hour on D-Day was 7:30 a.m. We were also instructed that, in the event of an emergency, we were not to consider turning around and heading back to base. The reason being that there would be thousands behind us at all altitudes.

"As we flew over the channel toward the invasion beaches, we looked down and observed thousands of surface vessels heading toward the invasion beach."

John and Edward were fortunate on that day, as both survived the invasion without injury.

John C. Albanese, a bombardier also with the 833rd Bomb Squadron, wrote of the attacks, "The 486th flew three missions on D-Day but didn't drop a bomb. The weather over the target area was so bad that the bombardiers were unable to make a visual run on their targets on the first two missions of the day and had to bring their bombs back home. Late in the afternoon, on the third mission of the day, we never left England. The weather grew worse, with a solid overcast to over 20,000 feet. We were unable to form our group and had to let down through the same solid cloud formation, and returned to the base. A lot of credit must go to all the pilots that day, as no accidents occurred."[103]

Not everyone was as lucky as the Rex brothers and the 486th during the invasion.

The 356th Fighter Group was directly assigned to Goxhill, England, after their departure from Grenier following an active period in the summer of 1943. They went on to support the landings at Normandy and the subsequent drive of Allied forces across France and Germany.[104] The 356th flew 413 missions between

October 1943 and May 1945 and suffered the highest ratio of losses to enemy aircraft claims of any Eighth Air Force Group. When Grenier is referenced as a final stop for American soldiers, the 356th is just one example of how dangerous the reality of war was for these young, often green air combatants.

A total of 4,414 Allied troops were killed on D-Day itself, of which 2,500 were from the US. In the ensuing Battle of Normandy, 73,000 Allied forces were killed and 153,000 wounded.[105]

Despite poor weather, chaotic beach landings, and violent Nazi resistance, the Allied troops dug in, pushed forward against steep odds, and persevered.

The result was the opening of a second front, diverting troops from the east. By June 11, with the beachheads firmly secured, more than 326,000 Allied troops had crossed with more than 100,000 tons of military equipment.

The first C-54 bearing wounded troops from the invasion in Normandy arrived at Grenier on July 8, 1944, which was chronicled in a later edition of the *Beacon*: "The wounded soldiers, memories of the flaming Normandy beachhead in their minds, were tenderly and carefully removed from the evacuation plane and driven in ambulances to the station hospital."[106]

Soldiers were given cigarettes, shaving razors, newspapers—anything to make them comfortable before being transported to larger hospitals. The same article explained that air evacuation facilities were standing ready at Grenier, but the base was only used for such purposes when the evacuating aircraft were not able to land at their scheduled port of entry. In that case, they were accepted at Grenier until they could be transported elsewhere.

Paris was liberated on August 25, 1944, and the war in Europe would end on May 8, 1945, known as Victory in Europe or VE Day. Soon the flow of traffic would reverse, with flight crews returning to Grenier from overseas rather than shipping out. On the one-year anniversary of D-Day, sixteen hundred airmen of the Eighth Air Force landed at Grenier on June 7, 1945. A few days later, on June 11, local newspapers described sixty planes, mostly Flying Fortresses, flying into Grenier. They returned over the same North Atlantic route that first took them into combat, making stopovers in Iceland, Greenland, Newfoundland, and Labrador.[107]

When World War II broke out, it seemed to Bill Soule, a young man from Massachusetts at the time, like something happening far away that he only learned about from radio and news reels. "Didn't really keep track of it," he confessed. But the end of the war would never fade from his memory. Soule served in the Battle of the Bulge, which began in December 1944 and marked Hitler's last counteroffensive attempt after the Allied victory at D-Day, when World War II appeared to be drawing to a close at last.

"Not too much to say about it," he said frankly, "other than that it was one of the biggest battles in Europe."

On December 16, 1944, more than two hundred thousand German troops sought to split Allied forces through an attack in the Ardennes Forest, an area that touches France, Germany, and Belgium.[108] It was a bloody fight but ultimately unsuccessful on the part of the Germans who had drained their manpower and material resources. The Allies resumed their advance and, in early spring, crossed into the heart of Germany.

Winston Churchill stated, "This is undoubtedly the greatest American battle of the war and will, I believe, be regarded as an ever-famous American victory."

Soule was in the 734th Field Artillery Battalion in the Army as a private first class. Asked if World War II affected how he saw life afterwards, he said simply, "It did at first. But then I outgrew it." He said of his experience overseas, "A lot of the Germans didn't like Hitler, but they couldn't do anything about it or they'd get shot." He said he thinks Americans today are forgetting World War II and the darkness of that period, at the risk of repeating it.

One of his strongest remaining memories that he shared from the war was when his infantry outfit overtook a concentration camp in Germany, about fifteen miles from where they were staying. This was Ohrdruf-Nord, a subcamp of Buchenwald.

"Eisenhower wanted troops to see why we were fighting. The camp was decimated; people were starving to death." When asked if it was worse than he expected, he said, "Yes, much worse."

Soule was present when Eisenhower arrived, marking the general's first visit to a concentration camp. Eisenhower would state later that he had "never at any other time experienced an equal sense of shock."[109] Soule said that Eisenhower responded by forcing the Germans who remained in town to dig the graves of the camp victims so they would be forced to look directly at the atrocities they had committed.

Eisenhower did something else as well: he immediately sent for newspaper reporters to record the scene at Ohrdruf-Nord where four thousand prisoners had been murdered as the SS guards fled.[110] Eisenhower didn't want the horrors of World War II to be forgotten, and neither does Soule. As he approaches the end of a very long life, he's motivated to speak of his experience to remind the world of how bad it was and what World War II was fought over.

"It was a bad time for this country," he said. "A real bad time."

After their crash in the heart of Nazi Germany and before their imprisonment, the men of the Toonerville Trolley were split up.[111] A few crew members had parachuted out of the failing aircraft, and all but the badly injured flight engineer, Ed Kolber, attempted to run from the German citizens that encircled them on the ground. Each member of the crew was eventually tracked down and made a prisoner of war. The officers were sent to Stalag Luft Three, in Silesia, now Poland.

The five non-commissioned officers of the crew, including Edward McKenzie, were shipped to Stalag Seventeen B in German-occupied Austria. McKenzie's escape kit was removed shortly after the crash, and he was warned by an English-speaking officer that, if he got too close to the barbed wire fence that encircled the camp, he would be shot. He was forced to wait in a cramped holding cell before being taken to an interrogation room where he was curtly questioned about his name, rank, serial number, and commanding officer, which he was genuinely uncertain of, having only met some of the crew the morning they departed for the mission. The end of his imprisonment came on a cold, damp April morning in 1945. The prisoners of Stalag Seventeen were woken and ordered to march, leaving the compound after about a year of capture. Many of the prisoners faced severe exhaustion.

"There were many nonedible items being shed also as men realized that they must unburden or collapse. Collapsing might very well mean death. When I saw a wool overcoat thrown at the roadside I knew that someone had really become desperately weak. He would be cold that night."

On this wretched march where their captors tried to guide them away from the advancing armies of the Allies, McKenzie's column passed a column of Jewish prisoners, none of whom appeared to weigh more than a hundred pounds. "We had heard rumors of death camps for Jews and other 'undesirables,' as the Nazis called those who were being exterminated. I wondered if this group of Jews might be on the way to or from such a camp."

As the column of Jewish prisoners moved past, an occasional *crack* began to sound, which he slowly realized were pistol shots that left a lifeless body in the road each time. If a man fell and did not get up, one of two men, clearly designated as SS by the death head insignia on their uniforms, would put a Luger pistol to the back of the man's head and fire.

As they marched, they fearfully listened for aircraft fire, as they were at risk of strafing from both Allied and German planes.

"On April 24, Cran Blaylock [tail gunner] and I, along with several others, observed our anniversary. Now we were each about fifty pounds lighter and a whole lot wiser about the glories of war and the nature of men."

It's difficult to conceptualize the sense of relief the American POWs must have felt one afternoon as they entered Braunau (the birthplace of Adolf Hitler) when a Jeep suddenly rode into their camp.

"It had an American flag flying from a front corner, and a captain was in the right seat in full battle gear. It stopped and was quickly surrounded. When the captain stood up, he looked ten feet tall. We froze into silence as he stepped out onto the hood of the Jeep. 'You men are no longer prisoners of war. As of this moment you are again American soldiers on active duty!' he shouted . . . What followed can only be described as pandemonium, with cheering, screaming, back pounding, and hat throwing. There were those who just stood and grinned, while others sat down on the ground and cried. What I did I cannot remember, but probably it was all of those things." Edward McKenzie was going home to New Hampshire.

On April 30, 1945, Hitler committed suicide after the city of Berlin surrendered to the Allies. From his headquarters in Reims, France, Supreme Allied Commander General Eisenhower accepted the unconditional surrender of all German forces on May 7, 1945, only about a month after Soule had witnessed the liberation of the remaining prisoners at Ohrdruf.[112] Hitler was dead, but President Truman cautioned the Allies must "finish the work" with a defeat of Japan as well. That would come later in the summer of 1945, with the atomic explosions at Hiroshima and Nagasaki.

About an hour southeast of Grenier, in Beverly, Massachusetts, preparations for this day had been in place for some time. In complete secrecy and unbeknownst to New Englanders, this unassuming oceanside town next door to Salem was to provide at least a third of the uranium used in the first atomic bomb, as well as Frederick "Dick" Ashworth, a weaponeer on the plane that dropped the second bomb on Nagasaki. The uranium came from a company named Metal Hydrides on the waterfront. Beverly resident Scott Cormier grew up hearing about Metal Hydrides from his grandmother, Ruth Nelson Rogers, who was an employee there during the war.

The story Ruth told over the dinner table went like this: One day, she was tasked with taking a train to meet an individual and was to hand them over a mysterious package. She had no idea what was in the package other than it was *very* important. Cormier isn't sure if her employer mentioned anything about being careful with the contents. That meeting took place (exact year unknown), she handed the package off to its unidentified recipient, and that was it.

But similarly to Manchester and surrounding towns, which were cratered by practice bombs and crashed aircraft, the story of Metal Hydrides shows how many civilian lives were changed by the war in unexpected ways. While Ruth Nelson Rogers went on to live a full life, the federal government would pay out nearly $2 million to former Metal Hydrides workers and their families in compensation for health-related issues as of 2023.[113]

World War II had waged for six long years, destroying the lives of millions, razing cities to the ground across the globe, and completely upending the lives of families on the home front, who mourned and fought in tandem with American troops overseas. And now it was over. Faye L'Ecuyer's sense of jubilation can still be heard through the crackles of static on a cassette tape at the Manchester Historic Association, recounting how for one shining day, people ran out into the city streets, hugging and kissing.

It's hard to imagine the joy and the suffering of that moment. How could the world return to "normal" after such a catastrophic event?

Humanity was changed forever by the atrocities of the 1940s; it marked a material alteration to the fabric of society. In the heat of the war, a new world financial order was established at an unlikely location: the secluded Mount Washington Hotel in Bretton Woods, New Hampshire. During what would later be called the Bretton Woods Conference, forty-four nations met to agree on a system of economic order and international cooperation that would help countries recover from the devastation of the war and foster long-term global growth. The conference produced the Articles of Agreement for the International Bank for Reconstruction and Development (IBRD) and the birth of the International Monetary Fund (IMF).[114] The IBRD would ultimately become known as the World Bank. Not bad for sleepy New Hampshire, but there was still an almost incomprehensible amount of cleanup left after the war.

There were many kinds of tasks involved with that global restructuring effort at the tail end of the war and immediately following its conclusion. For instance, there was the mail to take care of. Credited with clearing a six-month backlog of mail to American troops in just three months, according to the US Army Center of Military History, the "Six Triple Eight" followed a motto of "no mail, low morale." The all-Black, all-female battalion was stationed in Europe during the final months of the war, where they processed an average of sixty-five thousand pieces of mail per shift, for a total of 17 million by the conflict's end. The Six Triple Eight was disbanded in 1946, and the group of women received the Congressional Medal of Honor in 2022.[115] New Hampshire supplied a single member of the battalion in the form of Doris Moore of Portsmouth.

Doris Moore's nieces—Sarah Bodge, Gail Pettiford, Elizabeth Pettiford, and Doris Terry—shared a prepared statement upon the passage of the Congressional Medal Act, released through New Hampshire Senator Maggie Hassan's office.

"Doris Moore's service in the Six Triple Eight has made our family very proud of her," they stated. "Doris took pride in wearing her uniform along with her fellow sisters of color who served with her in the US Army. These brave women served with pride and fortitude as they experienced racial bias and limited notation. As a family, we are just as proud of her now as we were when our grandmother, who was a Service Star mother, displayed the Service Star in her window at her home in Portsmouth, New Hampshire, during the war."[116]

In the wave of military expansion driven by World War II, Grenier wasn't the only base to appear virtually overnight. After the war, the military began to assess what needed to remain in place permanently and what could be leveled, left behind. By the end of 1946, Grenier's operations were dramatically scaled back for a number of months to sixteen officers, one hundred enlisted men, and sixty-seven civilians.[117]

But the base had some spark left in it yet. In 1946, Grenier was given a new lease on life as training grounds for early New Hampshire Air Guardsmen and the 133rd Fighter Squadron was assigned to the adjutant general of New Hampshire on October 4, 1946.[118] The 133rd had its origins in World War II as the 529th Squadron, a fighter bomber unit that served in India and China. In April 1947, the newly formed 133rd was federally recognized after having reached adequate staffing levels.

With World War II over, the significance of Grenier in the community began to shift as returning soldiers considered what their lives would be like now that they were back home. Security was loosened. There were a number of air shows and public open houses on the base. At least initially, some veterans seemed eager to talk about their experiences. On June 25, 1947, Army fliers and ground crews from Grenier did a public Q&A. "One flier shot down [eighteen] Nazi planes, while others had impressive totals, too," read the advertisement for the event, which added, "Only the A-bomb and political questions will be banned."

The term "post-traumatic stress disorder" (PTSD) didn't enter the common vernacular until decades later, but there had been some advancements in military psychiatric medicine since World War I. Previously and at the start of World War II, the military believed that soldiers who suffered from what was known as "combat fatigue" at the time were predisposed to it before entering combat. As a result, the military screened for factors that they believed would make a solider more likely to suffer from combat fatigue and rejected them at the outset. This changed as World War II went on, particularly after the Battle of Guadalcanal. Out of the battle's survivors, five hundred marines were treated for effects like tremors, sensitivity to noise, and periods of amnesia, to the point where it became known as "Guadalcanal Disorder."[119]

A common symptom of PTSD is avoidance of things that trigger memories of the trauma. As a result, many World War II veterans did not speak frequently or ever about their combat experiences as time went on. Or if they did, as Dan

Kelley remarked of his uncle, it was usually a joke or a funny anecdote, a way of processing or diminishing the emotions that were less easily dealt with. For the soldiers who saw continuous combat, transitioning from the nonstop exhaustion of battle to a sunny weekend at Pine Island must have been especially jarring.

World War II was also an introduction to the concept of "total war," erasing the lines between civilian and military resources and casualties. A person didn't have to be in the armed services to experience PTSD. Ron Adams of Hooksett, New Hampshire, can remember playing at Grenier, sneaking onto the base with other kids in a contest to see who would dare to touch the planes. His mother worked at the hospital on the base and came home one night saying she couldn't do it any longer—she'd seen too many "basket cases" from the war and wanted to quit. Now that the war was officially over, many civilians and veterans alike were eager to return to normal life and put it in the past.

Throughout the 1940s, Grenier was also host to a number of ceremonies commemorating the war casualties. One of many similar news clippings speaks of base commander Colonel John Moore awarding the Distinguished Flying Cross to the loved ones of First Lieutenant Charles F. Dolan, Staff Sergeant Edward A. Adams, and Staff Sergeant Raymond A. Demers.[120]

It's possible to spend decades combing the backgrounds of those missing and killed in combat in World War II. Here we'll have a pause to learn about these three men, with the understanding that a full catalog of all those lost, even exclusively from New England, is not possible. Charles Dolan was from Charlestown, Massachusetts. He was married to a woman from Farmington, New Hampshire, for just six weeks before being sent overseas. In a raid against a Japanese airdrome in New Guinea, he went beyond his flight radius and sank a Japanese transport ship. Before failing to return from a single-plane mission, he'd already gone out twice with squadrons where he was the sole survivor. He has a marker in the Manila American Cemetery and Memorial and in New York.[121]

Edward A. Adams was a staff sergeant and a radio operator in the 90th Bomber Squadron, 3rd Bomber Group, Light, having enlisted in Manchester, and he was twenty-four at the time of his death. Adams was on an A-20 Havoc bomber bound for a strike on Wewak, also in New Guinea. The last contact heard from his airship by radio was, "Just south of Sepik River, engine vibrating badly. Governor out." In this case, the story doesn't fully end when Adams was lost. In 1970, a missionary named Reverend Daryl Schendel learned of a crash in a very remote region of the Bismarck Schrader Range and organized a party to go search for it. The following passage is part of his account of discovering the A-20:

"Our five-hour hike came to an end at a mountain ridge. I have no idea of the altitude, but it was very cold. Some of our men claimed we were close to the downed plane. My excitement was mounting. From the vantage point of the ridge we were able to make out the form of what turned out to be the wing of an airplane. Just opposite the wing a short distance away, we saw the fuselage and other wing. The main body of the aircraft was overgrown with jungle vines and bush. When I discovered the large USA star insignia, my excitement rose even higher. Here was an American World War II fighter bomber, we later learned, that had become lost from the squadron, and had crashed into the ridge. Our New Guinean carriers were not interested in risking evil spirit by coming any closer to the plane. Thus it was with all who passed by that spot. Consequently, everything remained just as when the tragedy took place."[122]

The searchers discovered remains of two crew members, a photographer and a gunner, and a set of dog tags in the cockpit belonging to Second Lieutenant Allen W. Garlick who was the pilot on that fateful day. The aircraft was a match for the Havoc that Adams helped crew. The searchers also discovered a live bomb "cradled in the arms of the tree root" and large .50-caliber machine guns with dozens of cartridges lying around the area. Schendel did eventually meet with the parents of the pilot in Minnesota. Adams has a memorial in the Manila American Cemetery and Memorial and also a headstone in Windham, New Hampshire.[123]

Last of the three men honored on that day long ago at Grenier was Raymond Alcide Demers of Haverhill, Massachusetts, who enlisted in North Conway, New Hampshire. Demers was part of the 761st Bomber Squadron, 460th Bomber Group (Heavy), which deployed to the Mediterranean from a base in North

Africa. Demers was a ball turret gunner on a B-24, flying missions against industrial concentrations in Italy and other installations in that combat area. On April 6, 1944, his plane was badly damaged while over an enemy target, and he failed to return. Sergeant Demers and three other men were lost, and his body was never recovered. He left behind his mother, Rena M. Demers, and four siblings.[124]

One unfortunate remnant of the World War II years at Grenier was the continuation of Grenier crewmen being killed in aircraft accidents between 1947 and 1949. A particularly terrifying crash occurred on August 13, 1949, when an AT-11 in a midair collision with an A-26 attack bomber fell flaming into a children's playhouse at the home of Mr. And Mrs. Harry Stone (705 S. Beech Street). Normally a dozen kids would be playing in it, but the day was too hot. A *Manchester Evening Leader* article from that date noted, "Three children narrowly escaped injury when the A-26 bomber involved in the tragic crash struck the earth and exploded near their small farm home." [125]

Witness accounts stated that the planes collided approximately fifteen hundred to two thousand feet over Manchester. The AT-11 came from Hanscom Field in Bedford, Massachusetts, while the A-26 had been flying from Andrews Field, Maryland, to Grenier. The AT-11 came down in the yard on South Beech Street, near the Highland School. The A-26 continued onwards for a ways, past the gaze of dozens of golfers at the Manchester Country Club, and then down into a field owned by Louis Martel on County Road in Bedford. Debris was scattered all over the neighborhoods, and the wrecks drew a crowd of about twenty thousand onlookers by the estimates of the day's newspaper reporting. The total death toll was four. The final body was located hours after the crash by Wilfred Samson who was walking in his yard on Gold Street with his son.

A visit to the neighborhood in November 2023 showed how much has changed since the crash. Lifelong Manchester resident Paul Scarlett was barely more than a toddler at the time of the accident, but he remembers witnessing the collision. He was able to point out the areas surrounding where each plane went down. Scarlett was playing in the backyard with his brother when he heard the sound of an airplane and looked up to see two aircraft.

"They collided and there was an explosion. I didn't hear it. There was a black cloud of smoke rising. There was a big ball of fire just underneath it and parts of the airplane going everywhere, especially one wing, just floating to the ground. And I really didn't keep track of the other airplane. It just kept going. The pilot must have still been flying it for it to keep going."

Scarlett has never forgotten the crash.

"It was traumatic," he said. "It's not something I'd forget."

His two brothers jumped on bicycles and headed over to the crash. Paul recognized he was too small to follow, but his brothers brought back a small piece of the windshield that they kept on the bulkhead in the basement of a family home for years.

From 1945 to 1947, the Army Air Corps downsized from 2.3 million men and women and seventy-two thousand planes to three hundred thousand members and ten thousand planes. President Truman and the majority of Congress were concerned about the costs of maintaining a large military.[126] Military activity was decreasing on Grenier Air Base. However, the base would see three more chapters of conflict before its final closure: the Korean War, Vietnam, and the Cold War.

The Korean War took place between the years of 1950 and 1953 when communist North Korea invaded South Korea and pushed UN forces to a perimeter around the South Korean city of Pusan. A UN retreat, counterattack, and strategic B-29 bombing campaign followed. The division of Korea into two halves was a result of World War II. The US and the Soviet Union agreed to temporarily divide Korea and oversee the removal of Japanese forces. In August of 1945, the Soviet Union occupied Korea, which had been under Japan's control since 1910. The US quickly moved its own troops into southern Korea. Japanese troops surrendered to the Russians in the north and to the Americans in the south.[127]

The rationale for entering the war in Korea, as phrased by President Truman at the time, was largely about reducing communist expansion, which US leaders were concerned would spread across Asia. At the outset of the war, Truman stated, "The attack upon Korea makes it plain beyond all doubt that Communism has passed beyond the use of subversion to conquer independent nations and will now use armed invasion and war."[128]

In 1951, the New Hampshire Air National Guard, based at Grenier, was called into federal service and remained active until November 1952. The 133rd Fighter Interceptor Squadron was activated for the Korean War, sending P-47D pilots.[129]

With World War II now in the rearview mirror, the world was entering a new era. US Senator Joseph McCarthy of Wisconsin had gained power and was embarking on a fear campaign against anyone with leftist political involvement. He and many other influential politicians of the day flew into Grenier to speak in Manchester. In November 1950, an assassination attempt against President Truman would be thwarted. The Atomic Age had fully dawned and brought with it a world on edge about the destructive capabilities unleashed by nuclear weapons. War had already flared in Korea, but the embers of other conflicts around the world still glowed, threatening to gain enough heat to reignite. With most of Europe recovering from years of bombing, the US and the Soviet Union emerged as global hegemons with dueling ideologies. This period of struggle known as the Cold War began in 1947 and ended only in the early 1990s.

Atomic weapons had been unleashed onto the world. Now we would have to learn to live with them and the new world order carved out from the devastation wrought by World War II.

Cold War scholars Lee Edwards and Elizabeth Edwards Spalding called the Cold War "the most protracted and unconventional conflict of the twentieth century." They added, "World War I and World War II were great sweeping wars that shaped our history and our world, but they did not match the length or the complexity of the ideological and strategic struggle that occupied superpowers and lesser powers on every continent."[130]

Korea and Vietnam were two "hot" conflicts that were closely interwoven with Cold War politics and cast a shadow over mid-century US, including New England.

Back in the Great North Woods of New Hampshire, Winston McCarty was preparing to return the call back to service in 1950 as part of the Army of Occupation in Korea. Once overseas, he was assigned to the motor pool as a dispatcher and a few other roles before landing in the intelligence department as a criminal investigator on the base. McCarty smiled a bit while recounting his job title, as he was only nineteen years old at the time. He said there were black market and minor criminal problems but nothing too major for him to tackle. His memories include a lot of restrictions in Korea on where the soldiers could go or how they could socialize, and he noted that the food wasn't processed or made secure from disease. McCarty was in Korea for about seven months before being sent home on early discharge when his wife gave birth to twins.

"I can't remember being in any sort of fear. It was mostly 'hurry up and wait.' To move large bodies of men around is time-consuming."

McCarty was sent across the ocean on a troop ship on four occasions. A lot of the men (all four thousand or so of them) were frequently seasick and a lot of time was spent waiting in various lines.

"Guys would get in line to go to breakfast, then get back in line to go to dinner."

Around this time Stateside, the role of women in the military was continuing to evolve. On June 18, 1948, the Women's Armed Forces Integration Act gave permanent status to women in the Air Force. However, women's roles were not as expansive in the Korean conflict as they had been during World War II when the military needed as many hands as it could find. The number of women assigned to the conflict in Korea was expanded from four thousand in 1950 to twelve thousand by 1952.[131] It wouldn't be until 2013 that all combat positions were finally opened to women.

But back in the years after World War II, Vicki Dyes just knew that she wanted to do whatever her sister Ruth was doing, and what Ruth wanted was to be like her aunt. Also named Ruth, this aunt had been a transport pilot at the end of World War II. One day in 1944, Aunt Ruth came to visit the family in a

Ford convertible with the top down and in her pilot's uniform, leaving behind a lasting impression on her two young nieces.

"I just kept thinking about that," said Ruth Dyes, now Mattingly. "She stayed in Florida and traveled all the time." A few years later, Ruth was looking into buying a new car of her own; she was shocked to find that it cost over $3,000. So, she decided that she and Vicki were going to find part-time jobs.

The two young women found work in Newburyport, Massachusetts, at the Chase-Shawmut Company doing secretarial work. They stayed for about a year before Ruth started getting restless. She turned to Vicki and said, "Let's join the military." But Vicki was too young to join, so it would be another year before they joined the Air Force together. They were sent to Lackland, Texas, for training and then on to Lowry Air Force Base in Denver in September of 1951. Ruth was twenty years old and Vicki not quite nineteen. Their original plan was to become flight attendants for high-ranking generals. That didn't work, as it turned out that there were only a few flight attendants for high-ranking officers in the entire Air Force. The sisters qualified as flight controllers, but Ruth vetoed that. She said she didn't want that kind of responsibility. So instead, they were sent to the gunnery and bombing group for aerial photography. There were about eighteen hundred men and twenty women.

"I would only go out with guys with nice cars," she said with a laugh.

In 1953, Ruth was told that, since the two women were with the gunnery and bombing group, they would have special permission to go on a training mission anywhere in the country despite the fact that women weren't usually allowed to fly. The one open option near home was Grenier Air Force Base, so they were flown in on a B-29. Ruth couldn't recall too much of the base, as the two sisters left to stay with family on Plum Island, but they never forgot that ride in the B-29. The only possible spots where the two sisters could fit were in the bombardier area and the tail-end gunnery. Ruth said of the ride in the bombardier area, "It was really scary, just glass underneath you."

One of the largest aircraft developed during World War II, the B-29 must have seemed like a futuristic silver behemoth.

It was the only time that Mattingly and her sister would fly into Grenier, but her Air Force career went on until 1955, and Vicki would stay for about nine years. Sometimes the siblings' decision to join the armed services did cause mild tension at home, a tear in their mother's eye or their father turning to hide the hurt in his expression when they left again. But at the end of the day, they were always welcomed back with open arms, and Ruth is adamant that joining the service was one of the best things she ever did.

"It opened up the world for me," she said.

Surviving yearbooks offer a window into the progression of time on the base. The 82nd Fighter Group was activated in 1947 on a peacetime mission of "maintaining pilots and crews on a status of readiness." A 1949 yearbook shows that most of the men in the group at the time had taken part in combat missions during World War II and held significant experience from fighting in Europe. Fast forward to a 1954 album for the 1610th Air Transport Group, Atlantic Division, and you'll see photos of Richard Nixon visiting the base when he was the vice president. Armed Forces Day that year featured a C-124 Globemaster II during Grenier's Open House. Photos feature a more racially diverse roster of faces, as well as a few women. At this point, the 9th Weather Group took meteorological observations for the area.

Photos from the yearbook show that it was clearly peacetime: soldiers going on picnics and taking part in parades and also helping put out forest fires in the White Mountains. One news clipping marked with the date of June 21, 1959, recounts how twenty-four Manchester cows, spooked by the sounds of an air show on the base, found a hole in the base's fence and marched onto government property.

Despite the reduction in troops and security at Grenier in the 1950s, it was still a time of conflict as global powers vied for their place in the new order established after World War II. Henry C. Schlecter was a Korean War veteran also present at Grenier in the 1950s. Schlecter grew up in Missouri near the

Mississippi River. He believed that the North Koreans would keep moving south and he wanted to get some military experience, so he signed up. Within two or three days after enlisting, Schlecter was sent to Lackland Air Force Base in Texas, then on to Wichita Falls after a week. He was assigned the job of air police and eventually sent over to Dow Field outside Bangor, Maine.[132]

At Dow, Schlecter mainly served as base security, guarding planes. From there, the Maine National Guard was shipped for a time to Manchester, to Schlecter's disappointment, as the winter weather was just as bad as in Dow.

When the New York state National Guard came up to Grenier for training, Schlecter reflected, "They had all these super brand-new jets and we some of these old propellor bombers." He said they still had P-51 Mustangs at Grenier at the time, which had once seemed so new and fierce. But now they were beginning to look outdated. Things were changing around the world. At Grenier in 1947, a committee of business leaders led by cigar manufacturer Joseph Epply was founded to lobby for the split use of the field for both military and civilian aviation. In 1950, Wiggins Airways became the first private carrier to return to the field after almost a decade of exclusive military use.[133]

The decade after World War II may have marked a transition to relative peace at Grenier overall, but on the gray Sunday morning of November 18, 1951, a new and disturbing kind of tragedy took place at the New Boston bombing range when the body of a young woman was found in a burning farmhouse on Joe English Hill known as the "Wigwam," which had been vacant for several years after serving as barracks for bombing range personnel. Fire trucks from Grenier and New Boston volunteer firefighters were summoned to the house, which was on government land behind signs that warned intruders to "keep out." Inside they found a deceased woman dressed entirely in black, half kneeling and half lying on her side in a very small upstairs closet.

According to reporting from the *New York Daily News*,[134] Air Force agents arrived at the scene before turning the case over to local law enforcement. In

1951, New Boston did not yet have a full-time police department, and so New Hampshire state police were summoned to the scene. The victim was burned, but the *Concord Monitor* later reported that pathologist Dr. Ralph Miller listed the cause of death as carbon monoxide poisoning from the fire.[135] An autopsy would later reveal that she was about six months pregnant.

At this point, a debate began to emerge amongst investigators. One opinion was that the cupboard space in which the unidentified woman was found was too small for her, a five-foot-seven adult, to have entered into willingly and then set a fire, with the theory being that she was pushed in head first and the door shut behind her. The alternative theory was that the woman had committed suicide, which may have explained her head-to-toe black attire.

A thorough search of all female civilian workers on Grenier was conducted, as well as all WAFs (Women in the Air Force, as they were named in 1948). Everyone on the base was accounted for, according to the *Daily News*, but base personnel denied in a separate news article that such a search did take place. Regardless, records from the New Hampshire state police show that Grenier officials were quickly notified and that soldiers from Grenier were sent to patrol the crime scene after its discovery.

A trickle of clues began to come in, including eyewitness reports from a ticket agent and bus driver in Manchester, who saw a young woman matching the description of the victim shortly before her death. The bus driver reported that she had told him she had to get to New Boston where someone was waiting for her. The ticket agent observed her reading alone throughout the day at a terminal, dressed all in black besides a single tan bag, which was not recovered at the crime scene, according to newspaper reports.

One item that was recovered was a packet of cigarettes with a New Jersey tax stamp, and so a search of soldiers stationed at Grenier from New Jersey was conducted, the theory being that the deceased may have had a connection to one of them. State police investigative files dated November 23, 1951, describe a set of dog tags that were found on the scene and given to Edward Boyle of the

Office of Special Investigations. Apparently, the abandoned house had garnered a reputation as a meeting spot for couples from Grenier Field.

A six-state alarm was broadcast describing the deceased, which was how she came to be identified as Gertrude C. White, twenty-seven, a bank teller from Trenton, New Jersey, through family and her fingerprints, which were on file from her work at a war plant. Relatives were able to confirm that White spent much of her childhood on a farm near the site of her death, offering some connection to the area. Her father, who was separated from her mother, lived nearby but claimed to not have been in contact with Gertrude for years. A few tipsters sent notes to the police regarding possible culprits, but the suicide theory appears to have pervaded. If the father of Gertrude White's unborn child was ever located, the publicly accessible state police files don't give this information away.

White's death made national news for a brief time but doubts about its cause lingered in the minds of some investigators for years. Like many of the stories connected to Grenier, perhaps there is more information waiting to be discovered.

CHAPTER 6

GRENIER BECOMES A MEMORY

BY 1952, AMERICANS WERE TIRED OF CONFLICT, something that Dwight Eisenhower was aware of and used to his advantage as the Republican presidential nominee in that year. Korea was costing troops and US dollars. Over 50 percent of Americans polled in 1952 and 1953 believed the war in Korea was not worth fighting, and 69 percent approved signing an armistice.[136]

"It was never inevitable; it was never inescapable," Eisenhower asserted in a campaign speech where he promised to personally travel to Korea and put an end to the war there.[137]

On July 27, 1953, seven months after President Eisenhower's inauguration as the thirty-fourth president of the US, an armistice was signed, ending organized combat operations and leaving the Korean Peninsula divided much as it had been since the close of World War II at the 38th parallel. The Korean War was over, but Eisenhower hadn't erased the fear of communism that would linger for decades.

A combination of heightened Cold War paranoia and development of new higher-flying aircraft resulted in a flurry of reports of visitors of different and more extraterrestrial kind in the New Hampshire skies of 1950s and 1960s.

At Grenier, several pilots filed reports with Project Blue Book, the Air Force's program to investigate Unidentified Flying Objects between 1947 to 1969. One report from 1949 was filed by First Lieutenant William E. Archbold who wrote that, while flying a C-47 for the 82nd Air Base Group, he was at thirty-five hundred feet when he spotted an object in a 45° to 60° dive "similar in size and shape to a fighter aircraft fuselage, silver in color, and of undetermined material." He said his eyes were first attracted to the missile from the light of the flame coming from its tail. "I was not fatigued; I had rested sufficiently and well the night before, and had done no drinking within a 36-hour period."[138]

Another statement from 1952 by First Lieutenant William I. Feustel, a member of the 133rd Fighter Interception Squadron, reported being in the Mobile Ground Unit at the base when he observed a bright comet-like object descending from space. The object had a tail and was surrounded by a blue and yellow haze like burning magnesium. "At the time it appeared directly over Manchester, a portion separated from the object and faded, and a few seconds later the main body of the object faded before reaching the earth, probably about two or three thousand feet." Feustel concluded his report with the opinion that the object was a meteorite or similar heavenly body.[139]

In 1961, a Granite State couple named Betty and Barney Hill made international news when they claimed to have been abducted by aliens while driving home one night on US Route 3 near Lancaster.

Patricia Dearborn, née Cullen, was ten at the time and living on a rural dairy farm in Tilton, New Hampshire. "It was a big topic in school; they all talked about it," she remembered of the Betty and Barney Hill incident. "We heard it on the news and some people thought it was funny, like 'yeah right.'" But at the time it took her an hour-and-a-half every day to get to school, and information wasn't always immediately accessible to confirm what was really going on in the world. "It did seem a little spooky. We didn't have the Internet. We didn't have a phone or a TV for a while."

In school she had a classmate whose family owned a farm where the cattle mysteriously died, but generally the other kids thought it was probably lightning that killed the cows rather than aliens.

But in between the talk of flying saucers, kids were expected to prepare for the very real possibility of missiles coming from the sky by learning to duck and cover beneath their desks. Dearborn remembered thinking, "That's not going to do any good if the Russians throw a bomb."

There are a few clear contributing causes to the flood of UFO reports that came in across the country in the 1950s, largely to do with advancements in aviation technology and a general unease about what else might come from the sky. Most commercial airliners flew at altitudes of ten thousand to twenty thousand feet, and military aircraft flew below forty thousand. After World War II, the US government never wanted to be caught off guard the way it had been during Pearl Harbor again, so the Lockheed U-2 was born to improve aerial reconnaissance against the Soviets. First flown in 1955, the U-2 could fly at seventy thousand feet and looked like a fiery object when caught in the right light.[140]

On October 4, 1957, a Soviet R-7 intercontinental ballistic missile launched the world's first artificial satellite named Sputnik and, with it, the Space Race. That same year, Grenier made headlines for releasing a balloon, the largest ever released in the US up until that point. It was two hundred feet in diameter when fully expanded and capable of ascending up to ninety thousand feet. The stated purpose was to transmit radio code signals on weather data. According to the *Union Leader*, the project was overseen by Dr. Alvin Howell of an Air Force Cambridge Research Center unit located at Grenier at the time. The balloon was to be set free for five days until an electronically timed device severed the gondola and all its instruments, causing it to plummet to Earth. The finder of the gondola was to be rewarded $25. "The balloon is often reported as a flying saucer, especially during the early evening hours," Air Force officials said. As the sun set, the balloon would appear to change color from white to various shades of red. The balloon cost about $1,000 and was meant to offer data on how balloons behave at high altitudes.

The balloon launch demonstrates that military leaders were continuing to search for innovative aerial technology and not always in the form of airplanes. In 1959, the practice area for bombers and fighter planes in New Boston was turned into a satellite-tracking station, causing weatherproof radomes to sprout like mushrooms across the hillside. Bill Harrell spent his days in New Boston during the 1960s on a team tracking satellites. He was there for about two years, from 1967 to 1969, but had a total of twenty-one years of active duty in the Air Force, then served another nine years in the Reserves before retiring.

He has fond memories of Grenier and of the area, although he doesn't miss the winters and now lives in Las Cruces, New Mexico. When he was first sent to Grenier, he was told, "Don't you get too fixed because we're going to be moving pretty soon," a reflection of the transient nature of the base even in its later days.

When he first joined the Air Force in the 1950s, Harrell was placed into the intelligence sector. "We were worse with the Russians then than we are today," he said. Before he settled at New Boston, he was stationed in Germany and ran a lab in Spain for a while.

Harrell also had a distinctive roommate during part of his time in the service abroad: musician Johnny Cash.

"At the time he could not play; he could not sing," Harrell recalled with a chuckle. He did, however, stay in contact with Cash and his first wife, Vivian, after their time as roommates.

Harrell said the remnants of World War II were basically gone from Grenier by the time he arrived: he never saw any planes dating from the 1940s while stationed there.

When Harrell retired from the Air Force, he went to work for the US Department of the Interior, maintaining the electronic countermeasures on B-52s.

"You can jam signals on B-52s," he explained. It was part of his job to prevent this.

Harrell was working in a laboratory in Spain when he became drawn into a major incident of Cold War history. On January 17, 1966, a B-52 and a tanker collided above the small farming village of Palomares, Spain, during a routine midair refueling. The ensuing explosion killed seven airmen and scattered four unarmed thermonuclear bombs across miles of coastline. It was his lab that supported the test equipment at the crash site.

One technician who would later develop health issues was directly onsite for some time because Harrell had sent him there as part of the emergency response, something he regrets.

"You can't help but make mistakes when you're a supervisor," said Harrell.

The Cold War may never have gone hot, but it wasn't without cost. Back on Grenier, however, the climate on the base had mellowed significantly since the 1940s. Richard Sansoucie looked forward to summer as much as any teenager. But unlike other kids his age who spent their time lounging by the pool or working a part-time gig at a burger stand, he spent his vacation months in the late 1950s and early 1960s on Grenier Air Base as a CAP cadet learning drill maneuvers. He could practically navigate the base with his eyes closed. Many decades later, he can still recall the shapes and spaces its buildings once occupied.

He would bicycle over to the base from South Mammoth Road and show his identification badge to the guard on duty to gain entry. Biking onto the military base and spending nights there didn't intimidate the young man; he was meant to be there, after all, and the air of intense vigilance that once permeated the base during World War II had died down, evaporating from New Hampshire along with the blackouts and the scrap metal drives. Weeds were allowed to thrive in household victory gardens, and the airfield, once a major staging ground for heavy bombers heading into the hurly-burly of overseas combat, now lay relatively quiet.

Not every part of Grenier was open to a young CAP cadet, however. It was the Cold War, after all. Sansoucie knew to stay off the west side of the base; that was still secret and off-limits. Although crews no longer departed Manchester to join the Eighth Air Force in its missions over Europe and North Africa, shiny F-86 Sabres gleamed on the field.

Asked if he ever tried to get onto the secret side of the base, Sansoucie replied immediately in the negative; he was a CAP cadet, and he didn't want to jeopardize his standing within the organization.[141]

Continuing downhill on his bike past the guard shed and towards a view of the Uncanoonuc Mountains, Sansoucie pedaled past the NCO Club, a chapel, a mess hall, and a movie theater built to entertain the troops. There was also a brick building that served as the base headquarters. The teen cadets would spend their nights in the barracks in the summertime on a side of the base that wasn't very busy. It was a great time, Sansoucie recalled. He got to use a flight simulator, and he met his first love (a CAP cadet from Vermont) on one of the summer encampments. The female cadets had their own separate barracks.

"The girl's squad in the CAP became regional precision drill champions," said Sansoucie enthusiastically. "Us boys were good but not that good. We were just all right."

Photos of the girls' squadron practicing on Grenier Air Base at that time back his words up. The young women stand ramrod straight and serious in their starched uniforms, with several photos showing a child little older than a toddler (the young daughter of one of the cadets and the group's unofficial mascot) at the front of the formation. The images are almost comical, but there's an intensity to them that makes them hard to laugh at.

When Sansoucie stares out the window of the 1937 terminal building at the airport today, built by the Works Progress Administration and now home to the Aviation Museum of N.H., his eyes squint in visualization of a past when the lawn around this area of the airport wasn't filled with holes because of woodchucks—it was an artillery range.

The buildings in which teenaged CAP cadets forged fond summer memories in the 1950s and 1960s are now completely gone.

Carl Stidsen didn't know Richard Sansoucie, but despite never having met, these men have something in common: Grenier. Stidsen, a volunteer at New England Air Museum in Connecticut, was a fellow CAP cadet from 1957 to 1961 as part of the tristate encampment at Grenier.

"All the termite villages from the war were still standing," Stidsen recalled of the time. "They were only designed to last for four years."

The CAP encampment wasn't small, either, with about three hundred or so cadets onsite. Stidsen said the dorms were all very similar, made of wood. Latrines were not separated, with no privacy walls or doors. Washing took place at a communal sink. Each barracks had a furnace, generally coal fired. There was no central heat, but having a constant fire meant at least one person was awake and on patrol in each building for fire watch, a legacy from the World War II days on the base. Beds were double-decker, and there were only two ways out of the barracks, making them difficult to escape in the event of a fire.

Stidsen called his summers on Grenier "delightfully primitive." He explained that all the KP duties (short for "kitchen police" or "kitchen patrol") were done by cadets on a rotating basis.

"It was my first year there, but I was sixteen and tall. The cadet squadron commander said, 'The guy who was supposed to be cadet sergeant hasn't shown up yet, so you're it.'" It was an excellent start to life as a cadet for Stidsen, as it got him out of KP duty.

Stidsen said Grenier was an Air Force reserve base at the time. Cadets flew up to the encampment from Worcester in C-47s and took a C-119 Boxcar home, loaded with sixty or seventy cadets and their luggage. He remembered opting for the window seat next to the propellers.

"They stood on the brakes and the plane roared, then started to waddle down the runway. I thought we were all going to die."

What got him into the CAP was a lifelong love of anything that flew. "I was one of those kids who wanted to be a pilot, forever and ever and ever. I loved airplanes."

He wanted desperately to be in the Ground Observer Corps program, an arm of the US Air Force Civil Defense service, which Grenier did have. But one had to be fourteen to join, and two weeks before his birthday, the program closed and the CAP was the natural next choice. "Whenever I could catch a lift

I would do it," Stidsen recalled of his teenage years, learning how to buff floors in exchange for plane rides.

When he got to Grenier, he was taller and larger than a lot of the other kids, so his job was to carry out the orders of the cadet squadron commander, organize kids, and run them through unarmed drills. Stidsen admitted he wasn't everyone's favorite person.

"I had a mutiny. Kids said, 'To hell with you,' and they tore the barracks apart. We had to return it to the shape it was in. Kids kind of melted away at the end of the encampment."

This left the older leaders like Stidsen with plenty of swabbing and cleaning, but it prepared him well for a future career in the military. He would go on to study European history at the University of Massachusetts, Amherst, where at the time every male had to choose between a stint of service in the Army or Air Force. Stidsen knew which signup line he wanted—he was Air Force to the core. And it turned out that CAP training helped him know how to drill. From there he went on to five years of active Air Force service and twenty years in the Reserves working with CAP. "When I turned sixty, they said 'You're out of here.'" But he never did get to fly for the Air Force. "God has a great sense of humor. Made sure one eye was out of whack. That 20/45 meant I couldn't fly. I was really kind of bummed out. The colonel asked, 'Do you still want operations? I have a special program for liberal arts majors.'"

And that was how Carl Stidsen went from a Grenier CAP cadet to serving over eight thousand hours underground as a crew commander for the Titan II ICBM missile launch site in Arizona during the war in Vietnam. Stidsen's four-man crew and others onsite kept their 170-ton liquid-fueled missiles on alert 24/7, 365 days per year, waiting for the order to launch their intercontinental ballistic missile to any point in the world, delivering a hydrogen bomb on target.

"The prevailing thought was that World War III was going to start any day. As Strategic Air Command, our job was to ride out the first strike and whatever's left, to ride out the war. My particular beast was nine-megaton warhead. We could toss that puppy nine thousand miles in any direction."

How does anyone deal with that level of responsibility? I asked Stidsen if he ever felt burdened by the gravity of the role.

"We were all volunteers," he replied. "I could say, 'Sir, I can't turn keys,' and *bang*, you're off the missile force." Stidsen was also very young at the time. "The morality doesn't occur to you when you're twenty-four. Plus, we knew everything would be dead and gone when we launched. We wouldn't live long enough to regret our actions."

He insisted that the Russians were on less of a hairline trigger than it seemed in the news at the time. A missile like that can't be launched without cause and very specific instructions—the only way he would have turned the key was if all preconditions were met.

"We've never been invaded, never been destroyed," said Stidsen, expressing a worry that the destructive quality of these weapons has become less potent in the minds of the public with the passage of time. The missile Stidsen worked beside could reach the Soviet Union and most of China and create a fireball three to seven miles wide, but when the citizens of the US don't commonly witness such things, they seem diminished and distant.

He said one part of the launch scenario in particular gnawed at the men.

"Our biggest concern was, if you got your order to launch at 3:00 a.m., would you wake up your wife and tell her she's going to die? Most people said, 'No, let her die in her sleep. The most merciful thing is to die quickly.'"

Stidsen is still dealing with some of the consequences of his service during the Cold War.

"The liquids in the missile were nasty, nasty, nasty—toxic, corrosive, and carcinogenic. We had 150 tons of this stuff onboard."

Today, he has a lung condition that may be a "long delayed kiss from the nuclear weapons."

Stidsen doesn't recall any World War II veterans on the base at Grenier during his time in the CAP there, but even if there were, he thinks they would likely have been reluctant to talk about the conflict.

"It was only fifteen years after the war, after all . . . Warfare is so against the moral code. It was a job that had to be done, but once it was done, we really don't like to talk about it. Nobody glories in taking another person's life. Nuclear war, that was so black and white. Nowadays, people have forgotten just how bad it can be. It's like a white elephant. When you get into the really, really big killers, you can't use them. This is a round world and the stuff comes back. That was true sixty years ago, and it's true today."

The 1960s had dawned with its own troubles. Early in the Kennedy administration, the president faced a situation that had the potential to escalate into a global nuclear exchange. In order to stem the flow of travel from East to West Berlin, Soviet Premier Khrushchev began to build upon and strengthen the infamous Berlin Wall. After having already lost face during the Bay of Pigs fiasco, Kennedy sought a swift resolution to the situation, relying on the New Hampshire Air National Guard to ferry supplies to West Berlin. A C-47 laden with equipment might spend forty or more hours of flight time circling the globe and returning to Grenier. The crisis died down after eleven months, but the Air National Guard was highly commended for its speed and service.[142] In the fall of 1962, President Kennedy activated the 902nd Troop Carrier Group at Grenier in response to the Cuban Missile Crisis, but after an intense six-week period surrounding that event, military activity on the field slid into a decline.

By the mid-1950s, conflict had erupted in Vietnam, initiating what would prove to be a long, unpopular, and costly war in terms of both US troops and dollars. By 1962, the US military presence in South Vietnam had reached some nine thousand troops, compared with fewer than eight hundred during the 1950s.

When Bob Lacroix was growing up in Manchester, security wasn't too heavy at the base, so he and friends would ride their bicycles over and lie right on the ground at the end of the runway to watch planes land. He always loved aviation, so when he graduated high school in 1964, he joined the Air National Guard where he worked at Grenier as a mechanic on C-97s.

"The Air Force had these gunships, AC-47s," he recalled of the Vietnam years on the base. "They outfitted them in Texas, flew them here, and from here they installed the avionics and the guns. And from here they went to Vietnam."

Lacroix clarified that just the equipment went over to Vietnam from Grenier. He said they did make an exception and fly troops at least once. His brother-in-law, a gunnery sergeant in the marines, was going over to Vietnam. He was told that, if he could find his own flight there, he could stay home for an extra two weeks. So, a group at Grenier agreed to fly a troop of marines to Vietnam.

In Lacroix's case, he did meet a few World War II veterans in Grenier's final days.

"Some of the guys in our outfit were here in the '40s and '50s when they were flying P-51 Mustangs. They started with P-47 Thunderbolts, Mustangs, F-86s, then became a transport outfit with the C-97s."

Harvey Cook, originally from Methuen, Massachusetts, entered the US Air Force Reserves in 1963 as a load master and was also there for the last days of military activity at Grenier Air Base. "When you're twenty years old, you don't listen to the news," he recalled. "Someone was like, 'That Vietnam thing is becoming a problem. Pretty soon they're going to start sending young people over there.'"

Someone suggested that Cook go to the airport in Manchester and ask about the Air Force Reserves.

"I was kind of nervous because I was a kid," he said, remembering how serious the man at the desk in the uniform seemed to him at the time. He was told that two support positions had just opened up on a flight crew if he could be ready to head to basic training in a month. Cook said he could, and his military career began.

Despite his initial nerves, he remembered Grenier as a friendly and welcoming place once he became used to it. Coming from Massachusetts, Cook said he really felt like he was up north when he was at Grenier. The base at that time was lush with pine trees that are now gone. Crew members could come up and stay for the night and enjoy fried seafood dinners on Friday nights.

"It was military, but it was very laid-back." Cook conjured a very different Grenier from the one where armed bomber crews had to sleep with their aircraft during the height of World War II. "We came up every weekend because we liked it so much."

There was one guard shack, which didn't always stop passersby for a check. Cook was very careful to state that this wasn't a signal of incompetence of any kind; there just didn't seem to be a need for the tense atmosphere that permeated other bases. Officers and enlisted men got along, and there were cookouts in the area marked off as a baseball field on base maps from the 1940s.

Cook has some fond memories of his military service, including time spent on a base in Bermuda where he rented a motor scooter and traversed the island.

"I think I realized I was very fortunate. The news hadn't been letting much out. They said they weren't fighting the war, but we were sending troops and said we were teaching the Vietnamese to fight."

Back at Grenier, the Reserve troops were tasked with taking some of the pressure off the rest of the Air Force, which was focusing heavily on Vietnam at the time. There were sixteen C-119 troop carriers on the base that were used for various purposes, including cargo transport and frequent night training flights. The C-119s were loaded with Jeeps, guns, and fifty-five-gallon drums of water, all attached to cargo parachutes. Being a loadmaster, Cook didn't have much to do when there wasn't any cargo on board, but he remembered exhilarating nighttime flights through the valleys of the White Mountains, flying at a lower altitude than some of the houses that were built into the mountainsides.

For some time, they were also picking up paratroopers from the 101st Airborne from Fort Devens, Massachusetts, and dropping them midair for training.

"We were told the paratroopers were crazy, and they were, absolutely nuts."

Cook said they would hype the paratroopers up with chanting on the flight out, some of them getting sick from nerves and the motion of the plane. Then they would drop them low, about five hundred to one thousand feet.

"Planes are hard to control, so the plane was bouncing all around. These guys are screamin' and hollerin' and throwing up. We'd climb altitude after they left, and everything would calm down. I wouldn't want to do it every day."

The flight crew of the C-119s were advised to stay clear of the paratroopers onboard. They were told that, as a 'joke,' some of them liked to grab the nearest member of the flight crew in the final minutes before a jump, taking the unwitting crew member for a wild and unexpected ride.

Cook also served on missions to carry freight up to Newfoundland, Canada, Greenland, and Iceland. Sometimes they would stop at Loring Air Force Base, an active base in northern Maine during the Cold War that was valued for being the closest point in the continental US to Europe. At the time, Loring was a Strategic Air Command (SAC) base that housed B-52s. Cook said they would park the B-52s "way out in the boonies" and load them at night with nuclear bombs. The armed bombers would cruise all night over Europe in case of an outbreak of a nuclear war.

On another occasion, the crew of a C-119 out of Grenier was on a trip down to New Orleans, a distance that pushed the limits of their fuel supply, when some wiring caught fire and the whole plane filled with smoke. Cook and the rest of the crew were told to get their parachutes on as they looked out over miles of pitch-black bayou filled with alligators and snakes. The flight engineer was feverishly tearing at the insulation, trying to find the cause of the fire. He succeeded at putting it out, but the navigation system had died and the fuel was almost gone. At the last minute, the crew was able to determine their location and call in to the tower to make an immediate landing. The crisis was averted, but it shows how quickly even a routine day can turn dangerous when you spend it thousands of feet in the air.

The C-119 wasn't made for performance, but it did inspire some loyalty from those who flew in it.

"You know if you have an ugly dog but you love it? That was the C-119."

Despite the tension in the world at large as the Cold War ebbed on, Cook insisted that Grenier was a place where the general atmosphere was one of comradery. The engineers all had "their" planes, which they would work on into the night after clocking out from their jobs as truck mechanics. They'd spend long hours tinkering, making sure everything was just right. Every once in a while one of them would ask Cook to help out.

"To sit in the pilot's seat when you're twenty-something years old . . . I was really excited to do that. I never forgot that."

When Grenier Air Base closed in 1966, Cook said the response on the base was one of surprise and disappointment. Suddenly, the base was being dismantled; life vests from the planes, parachutes, and tools that could be used for yardwork or camping equipment were given away to anyone who would take them. Cook speculated that quite a few guns were stolen in the commotion of those final days.

Cook was transferred to Hanscom Air Force Base in Bedford, Massachusetts, for the remainder of his service, which didn't have the same close-knit atmosphere as Grenier. The officers were higher ranking and didn't rub shoulders as much with the enlisted troops. When it came time to make a decision about reenlisting, Cook declined, although he admitted that he might have signed back up if he had still been at Grenier. At the end of his service, he took on the job of helping to bring home the bodies of soldiers from Massachusetts who had died while overseas in Vietnam.

"That was a little sobering," he said.

The 1960s was a time of downsizing across the Air Force as a whole. Grenier, where the engines of hundreds of bombers once hummed, was not immune. When the orders came to close Grenier Air Base, only two tenants remained: the 157th Military Transport Group, which was reassigned to Pease Air Force Base, and the 902nd Troop Carrier Group, which was disbanded. The final drill at Grenier took place in snow on January 16, 1966, and the final plane flew out of Grenier on January 19.[143] The control of the airport was now in the hands of the local government, with the control tower handed over to FAA personnel.[144]

Throughout its quarter century of operation, Grenier Air Base was a bit like a train station. It served as a hub where, every day, people would board transportation elsewhere. They might be traveling along any number of lines to different places. They could go through their days simply traveling to another station to drop something off and return. Other passengers might find themselves much further afield, having boarded ships or found new lines to carry them to places of great danger. The train station in itself was not always the most interesting thing; a train station is, after all, a departure point, a meeting place where people await movement into the unknown. Grenier was such a space, liminal when it was in operation and now completely gone. But the stories of all those passengers—all the soldiers, the civilians who ran the PX, the local children who biked to the runway to dream about flying—those stories don't have to disappear as well.

This book began with an introduction to Edward McKenzie, a young man not yet out of his teens, who was raised in New Hampshire and left for Europe with a crew out of Grenier one morning long ago. It also ends with McKenzie, as his story had a truly unusual chapter that took place much later in life. McKenzie not only returned to New Hampshire after his stint in a German POW camp, but he went on to serve again at Grenier during the Korean War years. He became an active historian of his home region and an author. And in the 1990s, a German historian named Klaus Zimmer reached out to him and the six surviving members of the Toonerville Trolley crew.

Before the hands of time wiped the slate clean, Zimmer wanted to know exactly what happened on that day in the sleepy village of Bubach in April 1944 when a fiery B-17 roared out of the sky. After extensive research, Zimmer was able to offer the American crew members an invitation: did they want to meet Hans Berger, the ex-Luftwaffe fighter pilot who shot them down? McKenzie said yes.

In May 1996, McKenzie and Tail Gunner John "Cran" Baylock both returned to the site where their B-17 had gone down. In remembrance of the cherry tree that saved them on that day by getting jammed in the wing, a new tree was planted.

In his own memoir, published in 1998, McKenzie described the surreal moment when he was introduced to the German pilot who almost ended his life over fifty years before.

"The old Luftwaffe pilot said to the old American air force gunner, 'Ed, it is very good to meet you.'" Then, with a smile, 'So much more pleasant than last time, eh?' He was a strong and healthy-looking man, and his smile drew my smile in return. As we shook hands, my greeting was similar to his. 'Although I didn't get to know you that day in 1944, Hans, it is as though we are old acquaintances.'"[145]

Hans Berger reached into a box and lifted out a model of his FW-190 fighter plane, explaining that he had made it as a gift for McKenzie. "For a moment the significance of the gift made me choke up. 'Now to make this totally unique,' I asked, 'would you be willing to write your name under the wing?' He turned it over and inscribed: 'In memory of our first encounter on 24 April 1944, Hans Berger.'" In return, McKenzie gifted Berger the replica of his World War II wings from his lapel, and the two men sat sharing coffee and their memories.

ABOUT THE AUTHOR

LEAH DEARBORN IS THE ASSOCIATE DIRECTOR OF the Aviation Museum of N.H. She holds a B.A. in Journalism from the University of Massachusetts, Amherst, and in 2019 earned a master's degree in international relations from the McCormack Graduate School of Policy and Global Studies at the University of Massachusetts, Boston. She worked as a staff writer at the Lynn Daily Item and has contributed to the Boston Globe, SOCO Magazine, The Town Common, The Chelsea Record, and other publications. As a writer, her goal is to tell stories from the past that would otherwise be lost.

BIBLIOGRAPHY

A BRIEF NOTE ABOUT THE SOURCES IN THIS TEXT...

A number of scrapbooks were consulted in the research for this book. This includes Bernice Blake's personal scrapbook and a scrapbook of CAP-related clippings in the Aviation Museum of N.H.'s collections, as well as a large scrapbook or clip book regarding Grenier news of unidentified origin in the collection of the Manchester Historic Association. A series of files were also consulted that were pulled from the Aviation Museum's archives and which are marked "Manchester Armed Forces Induction District" and individually dated. This is to explain that not all newspaper articles referenced have a clear date and publication of origin. Attempts have been made to locate this information whenever possible.

ENDNOTES

1. What McKenzie referred to as East Boston Airport was later renamed Logan Airport.
2. McKenzie, E. D., and Kenneth J. Kurtenbach. *Boys at war, men at peace: Former enemy air combatants meet to remember and reconcile*. New York: Vantage Press, 1998. Pg. 12.
3. Ibid, 14.
4. *Grenier: The War Years*. Photograph. Londonderry, N.H., n.d. Aviation Museum of N.H.
5. Hildreth, Tom. Grenier AAF, the Manchester-Boston Regional Airport in World War II. https://www.tomhildrethphotos.com/AIRCRAFT/AIRPORTS/MHT/MHTWWII.html.
6. "The Birth of the United States Air Force." Air Force. https://www.af.mil/About-Us/Fact-Sheets/Display/Article/433914/the-birth-of-the-united-states-air-force/.
7. "Air Force History in New Hampshire Historical Marker." The Historical Marker Database, July 12, 2018. https://www.hmdb.org/m.asp?m=119750.
8. Rep. *Historic American Engineering Record Manchester Airport (Grenier Field)*. Philadelphia, PA, n.d.
9. Breed, Allen G., and Randy Herschaft. "A Fire Destroyed Millions of Veterans' Records. 50 Years Later, Families Are Still Seeking

Answers." AP News, July 12, 2023. https://apnews.com/article/military-records-fire-veterans-2f8337c58bc87c10179a2cf6ee54136a.

10. "One of Last Surviving WWII Vets, 100, Reflects on Conflict." www.army.mil, June 3, 2024. https://www.army.mil/article/266245/one_of_last_surviving_wwii_vets_100_reflects_on_conflict.

11. Bunting, William L. "Historical Office Opened at Grenier." *The Beacon*. June 10, 1944, 43rd edition.

CHAPTER 1

Warnings in the Sky: The Years Leading up to World War II

12. "Hindenburg Lands; 'Spying' Is Denied." *The New York Times*, July 14, 1936. https://timesmachine.nytimes.com/timesmachine/1936/07/14/93523845.html?pageNumber=13&login=smartlock&auth=login-smartlock.

13. Shindler, Colin. "Hitler's Men in the States." *History Today* 71, no. 10, October 2021. https://www.historytoday.com/archive/review/hitlers-men-states.

14. Chapter 19: Between world wars. Accessed July 19, 2024. https://history.army.mil/books/amh/amh-19.htm.

15. LeRonn, A. "Aviation Has Bright Future Here as Adjunct to Recreation Demands." *Union Leader*. May 29, 1938.

16. Ibid.

17. Rep. *Historic American Engineering Record Manchester Airport (Grenier Field).* Philadelphia, PA, n.d.

18. "1934 Airmail Scandal Cover." National Postal Museum. https://postalmuseum.si.edu/collections/object-spotlight/1934-airmail-scandal-cover#:~:text=But%20crashes%20and%20deaths%20continued,died%20while%20flying%20the%20mail.

19. Hutchinson, Jake. "Grenier Field Named for Flyer Who Conquered Many Fields." The Beacon. September 8, 1945.

20. "Troop Train Brings First Big Contingent to Air Base." *Union Leader*. May 26, 1941.

21. "London: The Blitz, September 1940–June 1941." Historic England. Accessed July 22, 2024. https://historicengland.org.uk/whats-new/features/blitz-stories/london-the-blitz-september-1940-june-1941/.

CHAPTER 2

"Gives Practice Bomb to Child": The War Comes to Manchester

22. Rep. Historical Record: Base Ordnance, n.d.
23. "Vernon Wilkins Recovering from Bomb Explosion." *Nashua Telegraph*. n.d.
24. New Boston Historical Society. http://www.newbostonhistoricalsociety.com/joe.html.
25. "It's 'no Fooling' at Local Air Base." *Union Leader*. December 12, 1941.
26. "Research Starters: Worldwide Deaths in World War II: The National WWII Museum: New Orleans." The National WWII Museum | New Orleans. https://www.nationalww2museum.org/students-teachers/student-resources/research-starters/research-starters-worldwide-deaths-world-war.
27. Bernice Blake Perry's scrapbooks show that, for the war years, she developed a keen interest in sailing, but it never stuck the way aviation did. She would remain involved with aviation after the war until her death in the 1990s.
28. "Japanese War Machines of the Pearl Harbor Attack." PearlHarbor.org, February 11, 2023. https://pearlharbor.org/blog/japanese-war-machines-pearl-harbor-attack/.
29. "Why Did Japan Attack Pearl Harbor?" Imperial War Museums. Accessed July 22, 2024. https://www.iwm.org.uk/history/why-did-japan-attack-pearl-harbor#:~:text=Japan%20attacked%20the%20U.S%20Pacific,an%20empire%20of%20its%20own.
30. Taylor, A. J. P. "Preface for the American Reader." Essay. In The Origins of the Second World War, vii–vii. Athenaeum, 1983.
31. Hildreth, Tom. Grenier AAF, the Manchester-Boston Regional Airport in World War II. https://www.tomhildrethphotos.com/AIRCRAFT/AIRPORTS/MHT/MHTWWII.html.

32. “Unique ‘O.P.,’” July 16, 1942.
33. “Interview with Gen. James H. Doolittle.” National Museum of the United States Air Force^{TM}. https://www.nationalmuseum.af.mil/Visit/Museum-Exhibits/Fact-Sheets/Display/Article/196771/interview-with-gen-james-h-doolittle/.
34. 1LT Eugene Francis McGurl (1917–1942). Find a Grave. Accessed July 22, 2024. https://www.findagrave.com/memorial/56792095/eugene_francis-mcgurl.
35. Ibid.
36. All articles on local CAP history come from a scrapbook donated to the Aviation Museum by Dr. Henry Munroe of Pembroke, New Hampshire, who passed away in 2014 and served as an assistant chief of the Manchester Airport Fire Department for four years.
37. Civil Air Patrol. Senate resolution hails search and rescue participants, May 21, 2024. https://www.cap.news/senate-resolution-hails-search-and-rescue-participants/.
38. Highlights of Cap and USAF history. Accessed July 22, 2024. https://www.gocivilairpatrol.com/media/cms/Highlights_of_CAP_and_USAF_History__ABFCBED03EC81.pdf.

CHAPTER 3

WACs, Weathermen, and Bombers: Grenier and the War Beyond

39. Women’s Army Corps Veterans’ Association-Army Women United (WACVA-AWU). Accessed July 22, 2024. https://www.armywomen.org/wacHistory.shtml.
40. “Sub-Depot.” *The Beacon*. April 15, 1944.
41. “Research Guides: Rosie the Riveter: Working Women and World War II: Introduction.” Introduction, Rosie the Riveter: Working Women and World War II, Research Guides at Library of Congress. Accessed July 22, 2024. https://guides.loc.gov/rosie-the-riveter.

42. Vergun, David. "Rosie the Riveter Inspired Women to Serve in World War II." US Department of Defense, March 21, 2019. https://www.defense.gov/News/Feature-Stories/story/Article/1791664/rosie-the-riveter-inspired-women-to-serve-in-world-war-ii/.

43. Hazenfield, Everne. "Wac of the Week." *The Beacon*. July 8, 1944.

44. "Ex-Grenier Twins Now in England." *The Beacon*. July 8, 1944.

45. Wackerfuss, Andrew. "Women's Airforce Service Pilots (WASP)." Air Force Historical Support Division. Accessed July 22, 2024. https://www.afhistory.af.mil/FAQs/Fact-Sheets/Article/458964/womens-airforce-service-pilots-wasp/.

46. Join up? Where Do You Fit? Photograph. Londonderry, N.H., n.d. Londonderry, N.H.

47. "United States Coast Guard Women's Reserve (SPARS) (US National Park Service)." National Parks Service. Accessed July 22, 2024. https://www.nps.gov/articles/000/united-states-coast-guard-women-s-reserve-spars.htm.

48. "First Operation at Air Base Hospital," July 2, 1941.

49. Becker, Amy, and Frances Becker. Frances Becker Collection. Personal Narrative. https://www.loc.gov/item/afc2001001.24763/.

50. "Brief History of the Eighth Air Force." National Museum of the Mighty Eighth Air Force. Accessed July 22, 2024. https://www.mightyeighth.org/brief-history-of-the-eighth-air-force/.

51. Ambrose, Stephen E. The Wild Blue the men and boys who flew the B-24s over Germany 1944–45. New York: Simon & Schuster Inc, 2002. Pg. 23.

52. Ibid.

53. McManus, John C. Deadly sky: The American combat airman in World War II. Novato, CA: Presidio, 2000. Pg. 12.

54. Bio: Klinke. Accessed July 22, 2024. https://www.axpow.org/bios/klinketemp.htm.

55. Maurer, Maurer. Air Force combat units of World War II: History and insignia. Washington: Zenger Pub. Co, 1981.

56. “356th Fighter Group.” American Air Museum. Accessed July 22, 2024. https://www.americanairmuseum.com/archive/unit/356th-fighter-group#:~:text=The%20356th%20Fighter%20Group%20flew%20413%20missions%20between,the%20reputation%20of%20being%20the%20%27hard%20luck%27%20outfit.

57. Lumsden, Marshall. “The Invasion of Manchester.” *Air & Space Magazine*, January 2004.

58. Maurer, Maurer.

59. Warren, Harold Ray. Ms. My Spitfire Dot and Me. Aviation Museum of N.H., n.d.

60. Ibid.

61. “Fighting U-Boats in American Waters.” National Museum of the United States Air Force^{TM}. Accessed July 22, 2024. https://www.nationalmuseum.af.mil/Visit/Museum-Exhibits/Fact-Sheets/Display/Article/195991/fighting-u-boats-in-american-waters/.

62. Airplane Flying Handbook (3C) glossary. Accessed July 22, 2024. https://www.faa.gov/sites/faa.gov/files/regulations_policies/handbooks_manuals/aviation/airplane_handbook/20_afh_glossary.pdf.

63. “Ambassador Donald Blome Visits Kasserine Pass Memorial.” US Embassy in Tunisia, February 22, 2022. US Embassy in Tunisia. https://tn.usembassy.gov/ambassador-donald-blome-visits-kasserine-pass-memorial/.

64. Kraner, James Clem, Jane Diehm, David L. Rosen, and Sun Lakes United Methodist Church. James Clem Kraner Collection. 1943. Personal Narrative. https://www.loc.gov/item/afc2001001.91271/.

65. Dischner, Joni Lynn, Missouri State University, US House of Representatives/ Roy Blunt, Julie A Johnson, and Jeff Jack Johnson. Jeff Jack Johnson Collection. 1940. Personal Narrative. https://www.loc.gov/item/afc2001001.05395/.

66. Bagley, Paul D. Crosses in the sky: A true story of preparedness, discipline and training, and of a fortuitous aircrew during World War II. Durham, CT: Eloquent Books, 2010.

67. McKenzie, E. D., and Kenneth J. Kurtenbach. *Boys at war, men at peace: Former enemy air combatants meet to remember and reconcile.* New York: Vantage Press, 1998. Pg. 19.

68. Ibid. Pgs. 48–49.

69. Ibid. Pg. 68.

CHAPTER 4

"Our Safety Problem": Threats on the Home Front

70. "Escaped War Captive Lived on Art Here." *The New York Times.* October 15, 1944. https://timesmachine.nytimes.com/timesmachine/1944/10/15/issue.html.

71. "Home." Naval Sea Systems Command. Accessed July 22, 2024. https://www.navsea.navy.mil/Home/Shipyards/Portsmouth/About-Us/History/20th-Century-History/.

72. Cradle of American Shipbuilding. Portsmouth, N.H.: Portsmouth Naval Shipyard, n.d.

73. Dame, Lawrence. "$2,500,00 Manchester Airport Already Three-Fourths Finished." *Boston Herald.* July 17, 1941.

74. Kornegay Jr., Henry Jackson, Montana Pbs, Chris Seifert, and Christin Seifert. Henry Jackson Kornegay, Jr. Collection. 1941. Personal Narrative. https://www.loc.gov/item/afc2001001.76670/.

75. "Douglas B-18 Bolo." National Museum of the United States Air Force^{TM}. Accessed July 22, 2024. https://www.nationalmuseum.af.mil/Visit/Museum-Exhibits/Fact-Sheets/Display/Article/195870/douglas-b-18-bolo/.

76. Hoyt, Joe. "Battle of the Atlantic: Archaeology of an Underwater WWII Battlefield: Background: The Battle of the Atlantic: NOAA Office of Ocean Exploration and Research." Battle of the Atlantic: Archaeology of an Underwater WWII Battlefield: Background: The Battle of the Atlantic: NOAA Office of Ocean Exploration and Research, August 16, 2016. https://oceanexplorer.noaa.gov/explorations/16battlefield/background/battle/battle.html.

77. Busch, Harald. U-boats at war. New York: Ballantine, 1982. Pgs. 40–44.

78. "Battle of the Atlantic." Department of Veterans' Affairs. Accessed July 22, 2024. https://www.dva.gov.au/newsroom/media-centre/media-backgrounders/battle-atlantic.

79. "Two Serve 200 Hours on Anti-Sub Patrol." *The Sunday Star*. April 18, 1943. https://chroniclingamerica.loc.gov/lccn/sn83045462/1943-04-18/ed-1/seq-64/#date1=1756&index=0&rows=20&words=C+Pete+Sianis&-searchType=basic&sequence=0&state=&date2=1963&proxtext=Pete+C.+-Sianis&y=0&x=0&dateFilterType=yearRange&page=1.

80. Mireles, Anthony J. Fatal Army Air Forces Aviation Accidents in the United States, 1941-1945. Jefferson, N.C: McFarland, 2006.

81. Ibid.

82. Barracks and Bombsights. Photograph. Londonderry, N.H., n.d. Londonderry, N. H.

83. "Train Kills Soldier at Grenier Air Base." *Associated Press*, October 28, 1943.

84. "Believe Soldier Took His Own Life." *Union Leader*. August 7, 1941.

85. "Air Base Guard Shot and Killed." *Union Leader*. August 14, 1941.

86. "Soldier Charged with Manslaughter." *Portsmouth Herald*. September 9, 1941.

87. "Air Base Guard Killed on Duty." *Union Leader*. January 31, 1942.

88. "Negro Soldier Shot While on Guard Duty." *Union Leader*. January 19, 1942.

89. Delmont, Matthew F. Half American: The heroic story of African Americans fighting World War II at home and abroad. New York: Penguin Books, 2024. Pg. XVII.

90. Ibid. Pg. 37.

91. Eaton, Aurore. "A Dramatic Scene at the Downtown USO Club." *Union Leader*. January 12, 2021.

92. Wales, Solace. Braided in fire: Black Gis and Tuscan villagers on the Gothic Line. Tennessee: Knox Press, 2020. Pg. 383.

93. "The Bold Strokes of Edward Brooke." Arthur Ashe Legacy, February 17, 2016. https://arthurashe.ucla.edu/2016/02/17/the-bold-strokes-of-edward-brooke/.

94. "Powder Blast Rocks New Hampshire Area." *The New York Times*. July 4, 1944. https://timesmachine.nytimes.com/timesmachine/1944/07/04/86869674.html?pageNumber=21.

95. "Grenierites Interpret Blast Differently." *The Beacon*. July 8, 1944.

96. Ibid.

CHAPTER 5

Return to Abnormal: Dawn of the Atomic Age

97. "World War II, Korea and Vietnam Casualties Listed by State." World War II, Korea and Vietnam Casualties Listed by State | US Army Center of Military History. https://history.army.mil/html/documents/casualties/stcas.html.

98. Eisenhower, Dwight. "Order of the Day," June 6, 1944.

99. Baker, Keiligh. "D-Day: 10 Things You Might Not Know about the Normandy Invasion." BBC News, June 5, 2019. https://www.bbc.com/news/uk-48215675.

100. Reed, Adam. "D-Day Timeline." The D-Day Story, Portsmouth. Accessed July 23, 2024. https://theddaystory.com/discover/d-day-timeline/#:~:text=January%201944,-With%20the%20new&text=Further%20naval%20forces%20and%20aircraft,allow%20time%20for%20these%20preparations.

101. Issue brief. After Action Reports Battle of Normandy, June 2 to 17, 1944, n.d. https://www.dday-overlord.com/en/battle-of-normandy/after-action-reports/8th-air-force.

102. "World War II Flight Training Museum and 63rd AAF Flying Training Detachment." John Leo Rex, World War II Flight Training Museum. Accessed July 23, 2024. https://wwiiflighttraining.org/Cadets/Class1942/1942D/Rex_John.php.

103. Mission prologue. Accessed July 23, 2024. https://www.486th.org/Mssn/Prologue.htm.

104. "356th Fighter Group." American Air Museum. Accessed July 23, 2024. https://www.americanairmuseum.com/archive/unit/356th-fighter-group.

105. "Remembering D-Day: Key Facts and Figures about the Invasion That Changed the Course of World War II." *AP News*, June 6, 2024. https://apnews.com/article/dday-wwii-france-invasion-military-b02d03fa11f66767a521a3b01357a89a.

106. "Wounded Vets Landed Here." *The Beacon*. September 8, 1945.

107. "1,600 Airmen Landed Here on Anniversary of D Day." *Union Leader*. June 11, 1945.

108. "Battle of the Bulge." Battle of the Bulge | The US Army. Accessed July 23, 2024. https://www.army.mil/botb/.

109. Korda, Michael. Ike: An American hero. New York, NY: Harper, 2008. Excerpt shared by Bill Soule.

110. Ibid.

111. McKenzie, E. D., and Kenneth J. Kurtenbach. *Boys at war, men at peace: Former enemy air combatants meet to remember and reconcile*. New York: Vantage Press, 1998. Pgs. 252–253, 257–263.

112. "What You Need to Know about VE Day." Imperial War Museums. Accessed July 23, 2024. https://www.iwm.org.uk/history/what-you-need-to-know-about-ve-day.

113. Leighton Paul. "Beverly's Role in Atomic Bombs Often Overlooked." *Salem News*, July 20, 2023. https://www.salemnews.com/news/beverlys-role-in-atomic-bombs-often-overlooked/article_6d809956-2571-11ee-976b-b72d-4b057ca9.html#:~:text=The%20company's%20role%20was%20not,for%20the%20sensational%20atomic%20bomb.%E2%80%9D.

114. "Bretton Woods and the Birth of the World Bank." World Bank. Accessed July 23, 2024. https://www.worldbank.org/en/archive/history/exhibits/Bretton-Woods-and-the-Birth-of-the-World-Bank.

115. Kindy, David. "All-Black, All-Woman WWII Unit Awarded Congressional Gold Medal." *Smithsonian Magazine*, March 23, 2022. https://www.smithsonianmag.com/smart-news/all-female-black-battalion-in-world-war-ii-to-get-congressional-gold-medal-180979664/.

116. "Senate Passes Bipartisan Congressional Gold Medal Act to Honor Doris Moore of Portsmouth and Other Members of the Six Triple Eight Battalion." Maggie Hassan United States Senator for New Hampshire, May 4, 2021. Maggie Hassan. https://www.hassan.senate.gov/news/press-releases/senate-passes-bipartisan-congressional-gold-medal-act-to-honor-doris-moore-of-portsmouth-and-other-members-of-the-six-triple-eight-battalion.

117. Eaton, Aurore. Looking back: Grenier field springs back to life in 1947, February 15, 2021. https://www.unionleader.com/voices/looking_back/looking-back-grenier-field-springs-back-to-life-in-1947/article_35ca2049-d090-5fd3-948e-57d9cbf5032f.html.

118. Rice, John, Jackie Page, James Dolph, and Ronald Nadeau. Granite Wings: A history of the New Hampshire Air National Guard, 1947–1998. New Hampshire: P. Sheridan, 1998.

119. Malloryk. "WWII Post-Traumatic Stress: The National WWII Museum: New Orleans." The National WWII Museum | New Orleans, June 26, 2020. https://www.nationalww2museum.org/war/articles/wwii-post-traumatic-stress.

120. "Honor Three War Heroes at Grenier," n.d.

121. "1LT Charles F Dolan (1918–1943). Find a Grave. Accessed July 23, 2024. https://www.findagrave.com/memorial/55922856/charles-f-dolan.

122. Schendel, Daryl A. The edge of nowhere: Reaching the remote Kobon people of Papua New Guinea. Kansas City, Mo: Nazarene Pub. House, 1978.

123. "SSgt Edward a Adams (1920–1944). Find a Grave. Accessed July 23, 2024. https://www.findagrave.com/memorial/56786538/edward-adams.

124. "SSgt Raymond Alcide Demers (1923–1944). Find a Grave. Accessed July 23, 2024. https://www.findagrave.com/memorial/56363172/raymond_alcide_demers.

125. "Children Escape Death When Plane Crashes." *Union Leader*. August 14, 1947.

126. Rice, et al., Pg. 21.

127. "US Enters the Korean Conflict." National Archives and Records Administration. Accessed July 23, 2024. https://www.archives.gov/education/lessons/korean-conflict#background.

128. "Statement Issued by the President." US Department of State, June 27, 1950. https://history.state.gov/historicaldocuments/frus1950v07/d119.

129. Rice, et al., Pg. 25.

130. Edwards, Lee, and Elizabeth Edwards Spalding. A brief history of the Cold War. Washington, DC: Regnery Publishing, 2016.

131. Crissinger, James W., Air University § (n.d.). chrome-extension://efaidnbmnnnibpcajpcglclefindmkaj/https://www.airuniversity.af.edu/Portals/10/AFEHRI/documents/EnlistedWomen/women.pdf.

132. Jolley, Laura R., Larry K. Williams, Missouri Veterans History Project, and Henry C. Schlecter. Henry C. Schlecter Collection. 1950. Personal Narrative. https://www.loc.gov/item/afc2001001.107187/.

133. Brouder, Edward W., Maurice B. Quirin, Barbara D. Miles, and Christopher van Veen. Manchester's airport: Flying through time. Amherst, N.H: UBT Press, 2006. Pg. 142.

134. Norris, L. A., and Ruth Reynolds. "The Corpse Wore Black." Daily News. December 14, 1952.

135. "New Boston Victim's Funeral Is Postponed." *Concord Monitor*. November 24, 1951.

CHAPTER 6

Grenier Becomes a Memory

136. Memorandum on Recent Polls on Korea, June 2, 1953. Eisenhower Library.

137. Time. "National Affairs: I Shall Go to Korea." *Time*, November 3, 1952. https://time.com/archive/6608841/national-affairs-i-shall-go-to-korea/.

138. Archbold, William E. "Statement." Manchester: Grenier Air Base, October 4, 1949.

139. Feustel, William E. "Statement." Manchester: Grenier Air Base, July 19, 1952.

140. The U-2 & Operation Blue Book. Photograph. Warrenton, VA, n.d. Cold War Museum.

141. Not a sentiment shared by all young people in the Manchester area. Ron Adams recalled sneaking onto the base as a child, as neighborhood kids dared each other to touch the noses of planes.

142. Rice, John, Jackie Page, James Dolph, and Ronald Nadeau. Granite Wings: A history of the New Hampshire Air National Guard, 1947–1998. New Hampshire: P. Sheridan, 1998. Pgs. 38–39.

143. Ibid. 41–42.

144. Brouder, Edward W., Maurice B. Quirin, Barbara D. Miles, and Christopher van Veen. Manchester's airport: Flying through time. Amherst, N.H: UBT Press, 2006. Pg. 190.

145. McKenzie, E. D., and Kenneth J. Kurtenbach. *Boys at war, men at peace: Former enemy air combatants meet to remember and reconcile.* New York: Vantage Press, 1998. Pg. 30, 37.